D0788923

THE
PASSPORT
BOOK

THE PASSPORT BOOK

Edited by Nicola von Velsen

Texts by Philipp Hontschik

PRESTEL

Munich · London · New York

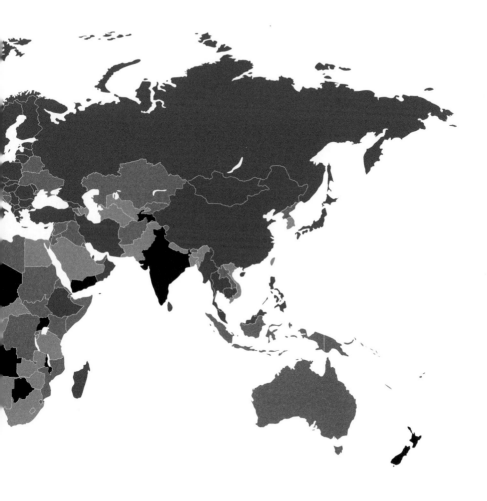

Countries A to Z

8

In Place of Instructions for Use

This volume gathers together the covers of passports from around the world in a small handbook. In our everyday reality as citizens, passports have become a powerful symbol in all countries. Holding or not holding one not least determines whether and where an individual may travel or stay.

We have therefore addressed the apparently simple question of what they all actually look like, what colors they are, what traces of use they show. Numerous people worldwide assisted us in our effort. We received pictures of the passports via private networks, and the quality of the illustrations varies accordingly.

We wanted to combine these "images" with selective information about each country and where in the world one currently is.

Many questions remain open between the pictures and the information—it is all the more exciting to delve into these questions *with* the book, pursue them, or to suddenly find the countries of the world collected in a pocked-sized format.

The entries for each country are structured in the same manner:

> Name of country and national flag
> Full name of the country

★ = Capital

🏛 = Form of government

👥 = Population, rounded up to tens of thousands

⌂ = Area in km², rounded

👪 = Inhabitants per km²

GNI = Gross national income

GDP = Gross domestic product

L = Official languages

↑ = Position in the Passport Index 2017 / Number of countries that can be entered without a visa, that is, with a passport only

The order of the passports in this book is oriented toward the geographic location of the countries and the continents in which they are located. Reading from west to east, they begin in the northwest and end in the southeast. All of the information in the profiles was derived from a comparison of various sources; the figures are rounded.

Details about political systems are geared toward their classification in the sources referred to (including the Office of

Foreign Affairs, EU database). However, how little this says about the subject of by the example of freedom to travel is shown, for instance, by example of Syria.

Population figures are based on information from the World Bank. Unless noted otherwise, the most recent available figures stem from 2015. The World Bank relies on various sources. Figures were rounded up, based on each of the latest censuses, assuming a specific birth, death, and migration rate—however, this inevitably results in certain inaccuracies. Even the results of censuses are not reliable in all cases, neither can migration movements be precisely established. We rounded the figures up to tens of thousands.

Area figures are based on a comparison of various sources. If external territories were not included, it is expressly noted. In the case of Denmark, for example, the land domain including inland waters encompasses just less than 43,000 km²; however, with the Faroe Islands and, above all, Greenland, the total area increases by more than 2 million km². Because the information in the sources differs due to various factors (controversial delimitation of borders, new surveys, etc.), the figure has been rounded either up or down: for larger countries to one hundred, for smaller ones to ten.

The population figure per square meter obviously cannot illustrate real conditions, since people in metropolitan areas live in close quarters, and in rural areas further apart. This information is only meant to enable a comparison between the countries. In Mongolia, for example, there are 2 inhabitants per square kilometer, unlike in Macau, with about 24,000 people per square kilometer.

The gross national income (GNI—until 1999 one spoke of the gross social product) of a country indicates its total economic performance in one year. The income of foreigners is not taken into account; however, the income of nationals working abroad is. The World Bank, on whose data the figures are based, calculates the GNI for each resident by means of the so-called Atlas method: using an average exchange value calculated from the previous three years, the GNI is first converted into US dollars and then divided by the number of inhabitants. This results in a certain lack of clarity; however, even so, it enables making a rough assessment of the affluence of the population of a country: in Monaco, in 2015 individuals had an average of 186,719 US dollars at their disposal— Burundi is at the other end of the spectrum with only 260 US dollars per person. Unless indicated otherwise, the most recent figures available stem from 2015.

Unlike the GNI, the gross domestic product (GDP) only includes in-country economic performance. We are citing it only because the GNI normally indicates the economic performance of a national economy. The data, given in US dollars, also stem from the World Bank and—unless indicated otherwise—from 2015. The United States has the highest GDP, Tuvalu the lowest.

The Passport Index allows determining how many countries a citizen can enter before having to apply for a visa. Germany, for example, ranks first—a German can enter 160 countries with just his or her passport, whereas an Afghan—Afghanistan is at the bottom of the list—can enter only 24. The first figure indicates the place in the ranking, the second the number of countries into which a passport holder may travel without a visa (visa-free and visa on arrival). Two organizations maintain these lists, namely Arton Capital (Passport Index™) and Henley & Partners (Visa Restriction Index 2016). The Index is listed on pages 438 and 439.

The official languages authorized in a country are specified in alphabetical order. With a total of 37 regional languages, Peru has the most official languages. In some cases, they indirectly provide striking testimony to the country's history: Macau, for instance, belonged to Portugal until 1999, and has since then been part of China. However, Portuguese remains the official language.

Finally, the short texts on each of the countries serve to provide a small view, characterization, or surprising piece of information about the approximately 200 very different countries gathered together in this volume based on their passports.

Everyone receives his or her passport from the country they are citizens of. According to the laws of the issuing state, the passport entitles them to transnational travel and in principle to return to their own sovereign territory. Besides the holder's particulars and details about his or her citizenship, it also has blank pages that can be used for additional official endorsements by the issuing country or for the entry of endorsements from other countries, such as visas, residence permits, or control stamps about a person's entry and departure. Dissemination of the biometric passport, in which personal details are recorded in electronic form, has increased since the early 2000s.

Besides passports, other types are issued, such as the official or the diplomatic passport. In some countries, there are even different versions, such as a temporary passport or one especially for frequent travellers with a greater number of pages.

Passports have a cover and numbered pages. Each of the covers bears the name of the issuing country and its national coat of arms as well as the type of passport. Property rights are held by each of the issuing countries. As a rule, the text in the passport is not only written in the official language(s) of the issuing country, but also in English and French (the language of diplomacy). Passports from the Apostolic See in the Vatican are the only ones in a dead language: Latin.

Since 1998, the International Civil Aviation Organization (ICAO), an agency of the United Nations, has regulated the standards for the production of passports, which are viewed as recommendations for national governments.

The dimensions of a passport currently comply with Standard ISO/IEC 7810 ID-3: approximately 125 × 88 mm (4.921 × 3.465 in.—thus DIN B7). In 1981, the member states of the EU harmonized their passports on many points, such as format and color (maroon–violet; Croatia is the only country that stands out with a blue passport). The biometric passport became the European standard in 2005.

The Colors of the Passports

The issuing countries can choose the color of their passports among the four variations red, blue, green and black. How-

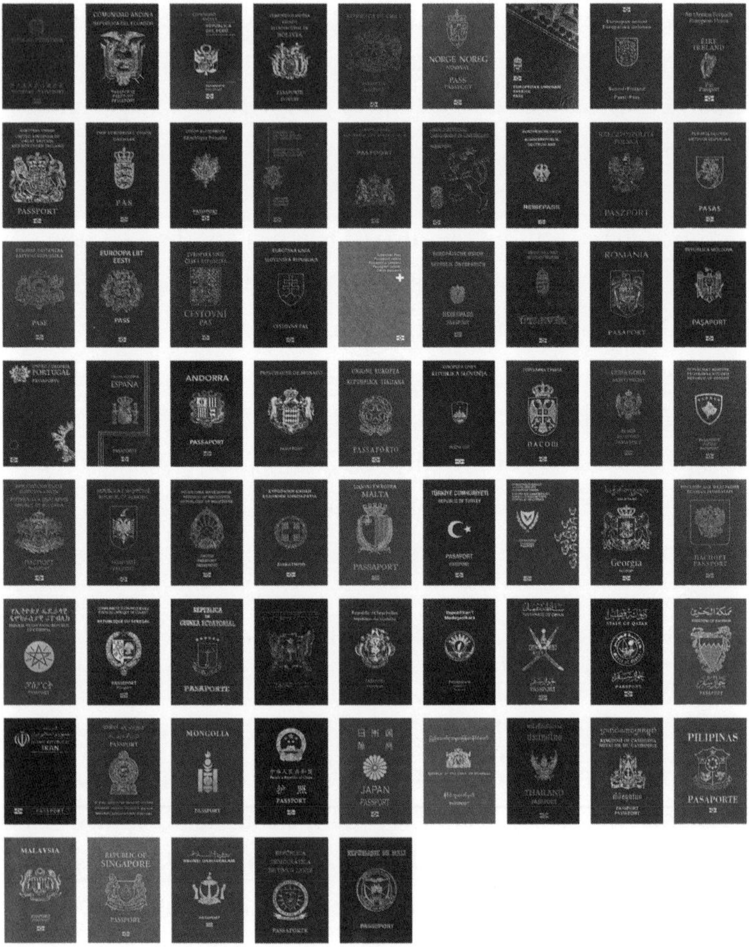
COMUNIDAD ANDINA
NORGE NOREG
PASS
EESTI
PASS
ROMANIA
PAŞAPORT
PORTUGAL
ESPAÑA
ANDORRA
PASSAPORT
MALTA
PASSAPORT
TÜRKIYE CUMHURİYETİ
Georgia
GUINEA ECUATORIAL
PASAPORTE
IRAN
MONGOLIA
JAPAN
PASSPORT
THAILAND
PILIPINAS
PASAPORTE
MALAYSIA
REPUBLIC OF
SINGAPORE
PASSPORT

ever, it sounds easier than it seems to be. While in the EU red became the standard color only in 1982, this standardization, meant to demonstrate unity, had already been decided by the member states of the EU as early as 1975. Some passports are intended to reflect the culture or religion of a country. Hence Islamic countries often have green passports; green is the color of Islam and often in their flags.

Dark colors are also very popular for passports. Smudges are less visible, and the national coat of arms, which is required to be imprinted on every passport, stands out better. Dark passports also come across as more official.

The Swedes and the Dutch have colorful surprises in store: citizens who have lost their travel documents receive a pink, temporary passport.

The color of American passports has changed multiple times: the first, from 1918, was beige; three years later it was green, followed by various shades of red, until green was again en vogue in 1941. The American passport has been blue since 1976 and thus reflects one of the main colors of the national flag.

Biometric Passports

Biometric or electronic passports combine the classic paper passport with electronic components that can be read by a scanner. Hence these are electronically interpretable biometric features in machine-readable travel documents. The ICAO has also been concerned with their development since the late 1990s. Following the terrorist attacks in 2001, the United States has demanded, and continues to demand, the worldwide standardization of the documents and the introduction of biometric passports.

The recorded information comprises a digital photograph of a person's face and fingerprints; it can also include iris scans. The aim of biometric passports is global applicability and readability, technical reliability and practicability. A key feature is moreover meant to be its high level of protection against forgery.

Nicola von Velsen

And without a Passport?

When Western sports associations boycotted the 1980 Summer Olympics in Moscow in protest over the Soviet Union's invasion of Afghanistan, several athletes from Germany nevertheless wanted to travel to the Games, so to speak as private citizens at their own expense. After all, they had trained a lot—and did not care two figs about politics. Then something very rare—and strange—happened: Federal Chancellor Helmut Schmidt threatened to revoke their passports, and by doing so prevent them from travelling to Moscow. In disbelief, many of them asked themselves if the chancellor was even allowed to do that (yes, he was!), and then brooded over the addendum: "This passport is the property of the Federal Republic of Germany."

This is just one example, and a rather harmless one at that, of how vital national travel documents are for individuals. Many of the refugees who arrive in countries of the EU from war zones and conflict areas have no passport or other documents with which they can identify themselves, and it is precisely this which saved some of them from immediate deportation back to their country of origin. A modern national bureaucracy is often only somewhat more flexible than in times of feudal rule: back then, one could only cross a border with the permission of the territorial lord, and today one can only do so if the host country's asylum provisions allow for it.

A Brief History of the Passport

The "passport system" has its roots in the Middle Ages, when imperial papers privileged travelers to receive board and lodging in the Frankish Empire. At the time, traveling at night was considered life-threatening in many places, and a shelter therefore guaranteed the resumption of the journey.

An irony of history: as a result of the French Revolution, in 1791 King Louis XVI is said to have attempted to leave France dressed as a valet. The revolutionary government consequently closed the country's frontiers. From this point onward, passport papers had to contain much more detailed particulars. On the other hand, the freedom to travel is regarded as one of the achievements of the Great Revolution in France.

Passports, visas, and exit permits have already saved many lives. Russians who fled from the Bolshevist Revolution were considered "stateless" until they received a so-called Nansen passport. This document, which would later benefit further groups of refugees from other countries, was filled out by the nation that admitted the refugee. From this point on it was valid for one year, after which it had to be renewed. The document's holder had the right to return to the country that issued it. One has to measure the meaning of what was often ridiculed as a "nonsense passport" against the backdrop of a Europe with Hitler Germany, the Stalinist Soviet Union, and fascist Italy. Since its validity depended on whether and which other nations recognized it—and in the end it was only 53.

The freedom to travel grew worldwide with the fall of the Iron Curtain. But this does not mean that all mortals and passport holders enjoy the same rights. Not by a long shot. This may be the case in border and business traffic among EU partners. However, the bureaucratic and often hardly comprehensible relaxations that have been achieved here in Europe are out the window as soon as one sets a foot outside the community of states.

Philipp Hontschik

No
Am

rth
erica

Canada

★ Ottawa

🏛 Federal parliamentary representative
democracy under a constitutional
monarchy

👥 35,850,000

⬜ 9,984,700 km²

👥 4

GNI 47,540 $

GDP 1,550.5 bn $

L English, French

↑ 6 / 155

Nearly all of the citizens of this second-largest country in the
world—whether Anglophone or Francophone—live near the
southern border. Nature predominates in the north—the further north, the more inhospitable.

United States of America

- ★ Washington
- 🏛 Federal presidential constitutional republic

- ⚥ 321,420,000
- ⬭ 9,826,700 km²
- ⚎ 33
- GNI 55,980 $
- GDP 18,036.7 bn $
- L English, Spanish (regional)
- ↑ 4/157

Shares the longest border in the world (8,891 km) between two nations with Canada and is situated like an enormous Double Whopper between Canada to the north and Mexico to the south. The largest GDP in the world. Leading cultural and military power in the "free West."

Mexico
United Mexican States

- ★ Mexico City
- 🏛 Federal presidential constitutional republic

- ⚥ 127,020,000
- ⌂ 1,964,400 km²
- 👪 65
- **GNI** 9,710 $
- **GDP** 1,143.8 bn $
- **L** Spanish
- ↑ 24 / 130

Many gringos think of it as South American because it is Spanish-speaking, yet it is unmistakably North America, and a big part of it at that! Hip, hip, hurrah! This is the only place to get authentic Mexican cuisine. Forget Tex-Mex!

Guatemala
Republic of Guatemala

★ Guatemala City
🏛 Unitary presidential republic

👥 16,340,000
◺ 108,900 km²
👪 150
GNI 3,590 $
GDP 63.8 bn $
L Spanish
↑ 39 / 110

Remains of Pre-Columbian history in partially undiscovered ruined Mayan cities; 35% of the land surface is forested, half of which is protected; until 1944 intensive cultivation (coffee, bananas) by the United Fruit Company (USA), capital punishment in force, last imposed in 2000.

Belize

★ Belmopan

🏛 Unitary parliamentary constitutional monarchy

👥 360,000

⬜ 23,000 km²

👥 16

GNI 4,490 $

GDP 1.8 bn $

L English

↑ 50 / 84

Only country in Central America where English is the official language, at the same time the only Central American nation without access to the Pacific. Every third citizen has African ancestors. Influenced by the Mayan culture, numerous off-shore coral reefs, abundant plant life.

El Salvador
Republic of El Salvador

★ San Salvador
🏛 Unitary presidential constitutional republic

👥 6,130,000
⬜ 21,000 km²
👥 292
GNI 3,940 $
GDP 25.9 bn $
L Spanish
↑ 36 / 113

Riots broke out during the 1970 World Cup qualification match against Honduras, and there were casualties; the conflict ended in a four-day "soccer war," the subject of which was the large number of illegal aliens from El Salvador that had occupied the land of large Honduran landowners.

Honduras
Republic of Honduras

★ Tegucigalpa
🏛 Presidential republic

👥 8,080,000
⌂ 112,500 km²
👪 72
GNI 2280 $
GDP 20.4 bn $
L Spanish
↑ 37 / 112

Nearly half of this nation at the widest point of the "Central American bridge" between the two hemispheres is covered with forest. Ten percent of the land is under conservation; small groups of indigenous people live in hard-to-reach regions.

CENTROAMERICA

República de

HONDURAS

PASAPORTE

Nicaragua
Republic of Nicaragua

★ Managua

Unitary presidential constitutional republic

6,080,000

130,700 km²

47

GNI 1,920 $

GDP 12.7 bn $

L Spanish

↑ 43 / 104

Atlantic and Pacific coast, the latter volcanically active; the pro-US Somoza regime was overthrown in the late 1970s; today—following successes in the areas of education and nutrition—the one-time revolutionaries resort to undemocratic methods; mestizos constitute the main ethnic group.

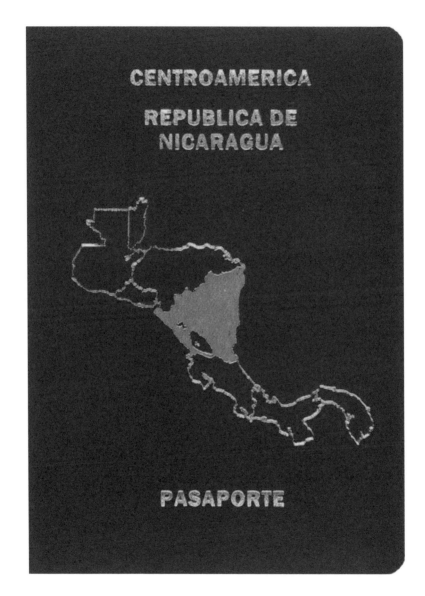

CENTROAMERICA

REPUBLICA DE
NICARAGUA

PASAPORTE

43

Costa Rica
Republic of Costa Rica

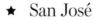

★ San José

🏛 Unitary presidential constitutional republic

👥 4,810,000

⬜ 51,100 km²

👥 94

GNI 10400 $

GDP 54.1 bn $

L Spanish

↑ 30 / 122

Situated between Nicaragua and Panama, the Pacific and the Caribbean, also called the "Switzerland of Central America." Stable democracy since 1950, progressive: regenerative energy economy, eco-tourism; neutral with respect to foreign policy, yet high crime rate.

Panama
Republic of Panama

★ Panama City
🏛 Unitary parliamentary constitutional republic

👥 3,930,000
⬜ 75,500 km²
👥 52
GNI 11,880 $
GDP 52.1 bn $
ʟ Spanish
↑ 34 / 117

The Caribbean "canal nation" between Costa Rica and Columbia; the Panama Canal connects the Atlantic with the Pacific, saves ships the circuitous route around Cape Horn, strategically important for the USA, upgraded in 2007 and negotiable since for ships carrying 14,000 standard containers.

REPÚBLICA DE PANAMÁ

PASAPORTE
PASSPORT
PASSEPORT

47

Bahamas
Commonwealth of the Bahamas

★ Nassau

🏛 Unitary parliamentary constitutional monarchy

👫 390,000

◻ 13,900 km²

👫 28

GNI 20,740 $

GDP 8.9 bn $

L English

↑ 23 / 131

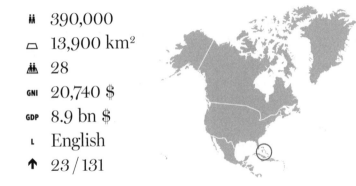

The 700 islands and 2,400 coral reefs in the Atlantic belong to the Caribbean or Central America, only 30 of the islands are inhabited. "Tax haven"; subsistence fishing and farming; primary source of income tourism, cruises with American retirees from Florida.

Cuba
Republic of Cuba

- ★ Havanna
- 🏛 Unitary Marxist-Leninistone-party state

- 👥 11,390,000
- ⬜ 110,900 km²
- 👪 103
- GNI 5,880 $ (2011)
- GDP 77.1 bn $ (2013)
- L Spanish
- ↑ 66 / 60

During the dictatorship, American brothels and gambling casinos; socialist revolutionary regime under Fidel Castro since 1950, strong link to the USSR; the US continues to maintain a military base on the island. Sources of income: tourism, cane sugar, cigars, and rum.

REPUBLICA DE CUBA

PASAPORTE

Jamaica

★ Kingston
🏛 Unitary parliamentary constitutional monarchy

👥 2,730,000
◺ 11,000 km²
👥 248
GNI 5050 $
GDP 14.3 bn $
L English
↑ 51 / 78

Caribbean island south of Cuba, exports: bauxite, allspice, cane sugar, citrus fruit, bananas, coffee. Capital: Kingston (population 950,000), main religion: "evangelical" Christians, better known as "Rastafarians," worship deceased Ethiopian Emperor Haile Selassie.

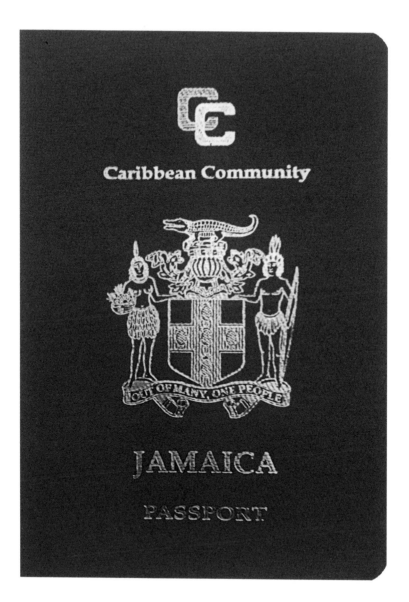

Caribbean Community

OUT OF MANY, ONE PEOPLE

JAMAICA

PASSPORT

Haiti
Republic of Haiti

★ Port-au-Prince
🏛 Unitary semi-presidential republic

👥 10,710,000
⬭ 27,800 km²
👪 385
GNI 810 $
GDP 8.8 bn $
L Creole, French
↑ 72 / 54

Shares the Caribbean island of Hispaniola with the Domini-
can Republic. Once Latin America's wealthiest country, today
its poorhouse, earthquakes, corruption; political unrest. Three
million citizens have immigrated since 1990, about ten million
remain.

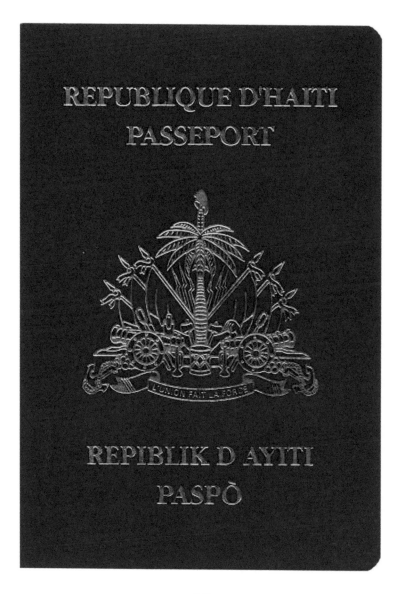

Dominican Republic

★ Santo Domingo
🏛 Unitary presidential republic

👥 10,530,000
⬜ 48,700 km²
👪 216
GNI 6,240 $
GDP 68.1 bn $
L Spanish
↑ 66 / 60

Popular vacation island, but often stricken by natural disasters, tropical climate, one third of the land area is under conservation, many of the local people of Haitian ancestry. Seventy percent of the inhabitants are the descendants of slaves from Africa.

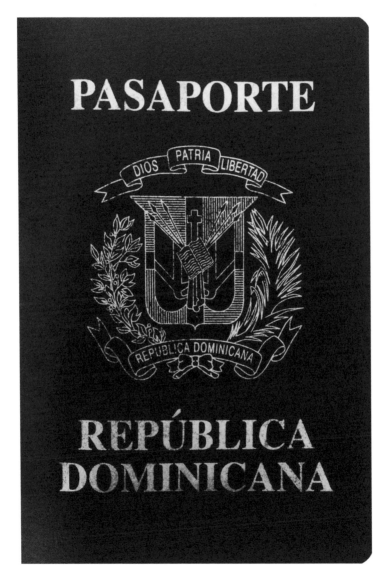

Saint Kitts and Nevis
Federation of Saint Kitts and Nevis

★ Basseterre
🏛 Federal parliamentary constitutional monarchy

👥 60,000
⬠ 270 km²
👥 222
GNI 15,060 $
GDP 0.9 bn $
L English
↑ 28 / 125

One of the 12 smallest nations in the world, belongs to the "Lesser Antilles," the UN, and the Commonwealth; trade winds allay the tropical climate; besides English, Creole dialects; predominantly Christian-Anglican.

Antigua and Barbuda

★ St. John's

🏛 Parliamentary democracy
under constitutional monarchy

👥 90,000

◠ 440 km²

👥 205

GNI 13,270 $

GDP 1.3 bn $

L English

↑ 27 / 126

Independent Commonwealth state comprising two islands
between the North Atlantic and the Caribbean; populated
since 10,000 BCE by Ciboney Indians. Columbus landed on
Antigua in 1493, thereafter slave islands; ship's flag considered
flag of convenience for shipping companies.

CARIBBEAN COMMUNITY

ANTIGUA AND BARBUDA

PASSPORT

Dominica
Commonwealth of Dominica

★ Roseau
🏛 Unitary parliamentary republic

👬 70,000
⬭ 750 km²
👪 93
GNI 6,800 $
GDP 5 bn $
L English
↑ 36 / 113

An unusually large number of centenarians live here (1 out of 3,450, compare Germany: 1 out of 12,200), rare for lesser-developed regions; reason not known.

CARIBBEAN COMMUNITY

COMMONWEALTH OF
DOMINICA

PASSPORT

Saint Lucia

★ Castries
🏛 Parliamentary democracy
under constitutional monarchy

👥 190,000
⬭ 620 km²
👪 306
GNI 7,350 $
GDP 1.4 bn $
L English
↑ 32 / 120

West Indian island, current population stems from black
Africans transported here as slaves in colonial times. Discovered by Columbus during his third voyage, ca. 1500; went
from being a sugar island to a banana island in the mid-20th
century.

Saint Vincent and the Grenadines

★ Kingstown

🏛 Parliamentary democracy und constitutional monarchy

👥 110,000

⌂ 390 km²

👪 282

GNI 6,630 $

GDP 7 bn $

L English

↑ 30 / 122

West Indian Caribbean island (St. Vincent) and 32 of the northern "Grenadines," colonial rulers created cane sugar plantations on the basis of slavery. "Bounty" commander Bligh brought breadfruit for reasons of population growth; movie set for *Pirates of the Caribbean*.

CARIBBEAN COMMUNITY

ST. VINCENT AND THE GRENADINES

PASSPORT
PASAPORTE
PASSEPORT

Grenada

★ Saint George's

🏛 Parlamentary democracy under constitutional monarchy

👥 110,000

⌂ 350 km²

👥 314

GNI 8,650 $

GDP 1 bn $

L English

↑ 34 / 117

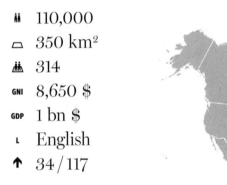

Main island of Grenada and further islands of the "Grenadines"; the USA intervened militarily in 1983 against the protest of the UN, the UK, and Canada. One of the grounds: "security of American citizens on the island" (students); more plausible: fear of losing influence in the Caribbean.

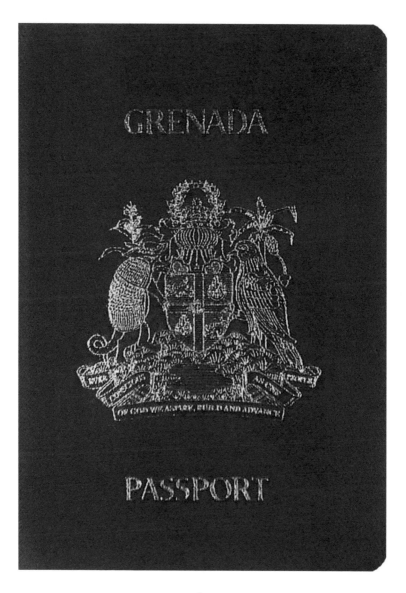

Barbados

★ Bridgetown
🏛 Unitary parliamentary constitutional monarchy

👥 280,000
◻ 430 km²
👪 651
GNI 14,510 $
GDP 4.4 bn $
L English
↑ 21 / 134

The EU classifies Barbados as a "tax haven"; formerly dependent on sugar, rum, and syrup, today active in the areas of tourism and oil production; third oldest parliament in the Commonwealth. In 1652, London pledged freedom of religion, constitutionality, and independence in the Charter of Barbados.

So Am

uth
·
erica

Colombia
Republic of Columbia

★ Bogotá
🏛 Unitary presidential constitutional republic

👥 48,230,000
◻ 1,141,700 km²
⛰ 42
GNI 7,140 $
GDP 292.1 bn $
L Spanish
↑ 42 / 105

Caribbean and Pacific coasts, parts of the Andes and Amazonia; the capital Bogotá and Medellín destabilized for years by drug cartels and the fight against them; in addition groups of rebels (FARC), recent progress in establishing peace and reducing poverty.

REPUBLICA DE COLOMBIA

PASAPORTE
PASSPORT - PASSEPORT

Venezuela
Bolivarian Republic Venezuela

★ Caracas

🏛 Federal presidential
constitutional republic

👥 31,110,000

⬭ 912,000 km²

👪 34

GNI 11,780 $ (2013)

GDP 371.3 bn $ (2013)

L Spanish and
31 regional languages

↑ 31 / 121

Oil industry largest employer, politically unstable, pro-democracy movements are fiercely combated. Coastline totals 2,800 km, a lot of fishing, 40 % of the land area is covered with forest but difficult to access; used little, main source of income is raising cattle.

Trinidad and Tobago
Republic of Trinidad and Tobago

★ Port of Spain
🏛 Unitary parliamentary
constitutional republic

👥 1,360,000
⬠ 5130 km²
👥 265
GNI 17,640 $
GDP 23.6 bn $
L English
↑ 29 / 123

Named "Trinidad" (trinity) by Columbus personally, "Tobago" from the Spanish word for tobacco. Bountiful Caribbean biodiversity, one national park, five regions under conservation; indigenous Arawak Indians died out in ca. 1800, long a slave and plantation island.

Guyana
Co-operative Republic of Guyana

★ Georgetown
🏛 Unitary presidential republic

👥 770,000
⬭ 215,000 km²
👪 4
GNI 4,090 $
GDP 3.2 bn $
L English
↑ 52 / 76

Name of the mountain range at the border to Venezuela and Brazil; agriculture: rice, sugar, coconut, citrus fruit; tropical climate, would be seriously affected by a rise in the sea level; predominantly Christian, indigenous peoples in the uplands have their own religions.

Suriname
Republic of Suriname

★ Paramaribo
🏛 Unitary parliamentary republic

👥 540,000
⬯ 163,800 km²
👪 3
GNI 9,360 $
GDP 5.2 bn $
L Dutch
↑ 57 / 69

Smallest nation in South America on the northeastern coast of the Atlantic. Came under Dutch rule in ca. 1700; has maintained close ties with the former colonial power since independence in 1975; Dutch still the lingua franca.

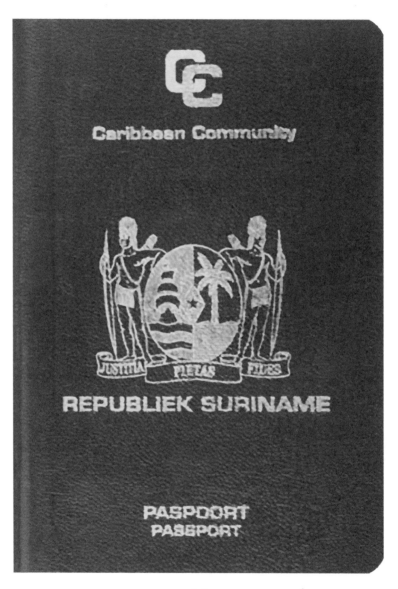

Ecuador
Republic of Ecuador

★ Quito

🏛 Unitary presidential constitutional
republic

👥 16,140,000

◻ 256,400 km²

👪 63

GNI 6,030 $

GDP 100.2 bn $

L Spanish and
regional languages

↑ 52 / 76

Its capital of Quito is situated at an altitude of 2,850 m (Andes);
the largest city, Guayaquil, in the level country of the Pacific
coast; Galápagos Islands ca. 1,000 km from the Pacific coast;
oil and flower industry, massive social inequality.

COMUNIDAD ANDINA

REPUBLICA DEL ECUADOR

PASAPORTE
PASSPORT
PASSEPORT

Peru
Republic of Peru

★ Lima

🏛 Unitary presidential constitutional republic

👥 31,380,000

⏛ 1,285,200 km²

👥 24

GNI 6,130 $

GDP 189.1 bn $

L Spanish and
37 regional languages

↑ 32 / 120

The potato gene bank in the capital of Lima cites 4,000 culti-vated varieties. The remains of the ancient Inca city at Machu Picchu is South America's most important travel destination, lots of wild nature, the Amazon and tributaries, Lake Titicaca; major shadow economy. Guinea pigs = meat dish.

Brazil
Federative Republic of Brazil

★ Brasília
🏛 Federal presidential constitutional republic

👥 207,850,000
◻ 8,547,400 km²
👪 24
GNI 9,850 $
GDP 1774.7 bn $
L Portuguese
↑ 15 / 144

Largest territorial state in South America, local language
Portuguese; fifth-largest country in the world, megacities
with sprawling slums; major soccer power with five World
Cup titles. Economically diverse: several regions meet EU
standards, others far below the poverty line.

Bolivia
Plurinational State of Bolivia

★ Sucre
🏛 Unitary presidential constitutional republic

👥 10,730,000
◳ 1,098,600 km²
👥 10
GNI 3,000 $
GDP 33 bn $
L Spanish and
36 regional languages
↑ 58 / 68

"Multinational," 37 (!) official languages, one half of the population indigenous, most live in the uplands; 30 % of the inhabitants are mestizos, the remainder white immigrants. Contains part of lake Titicaca. Named after Simon Bolivar, who won independence in 1825.

COMUNIDAD ANDINA
ESTADO
PLURINACIONAL DE
BOLIVIA

PASAPORTE
PASSPORT

Paraguay
Republic of Paraguay

★ Asunción

🏛 Unitary presidential constitutional republic

👥 6,640,000

⬜ 406,800 km²

👪 16

GNI 4,190 $

GDP 27.1 bn $

L Guaraní, Spanish

↑ 34 / 117

Not Spanish but Guarani is the strongest language group; less marked immigration from Europe than from Brazil and Argentina. Under dictator Stroessner (1954–89), who was of German descent, a great deal of immigrants from Germany; current a "semi-free" country.

REPÚBLICA DEL PARAGUAY

PASAPORTE

Chile
Republic of Chile

★ Santiago de Chile

🏛 Unitary presidential constitutional republic

👥 17,950,000

⬜ 756,100 km²

⛰ 24

GNI 14,100 $

GDP 240.8 bn $

L Spanish

↑ 17 / 141

Situated along the Pacific coast of the "South American Southern Cone," access to the Atlantic via Cape Horn. President Allende (from 1970) overthrown in a bloody putsch by the Pinochet military junta, then dictatorship, processing the past continues, today a functional presidential democracy.

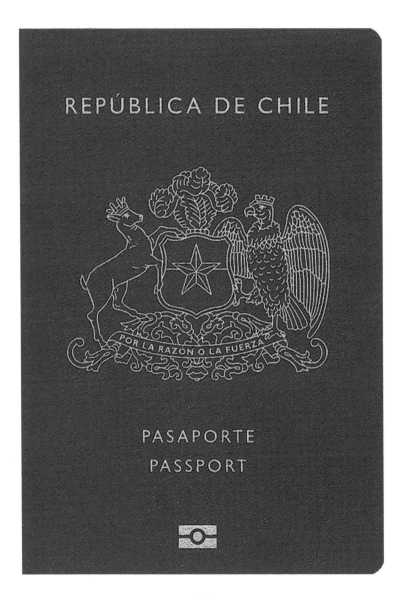

REPÚBLICA DE CHILE

POR LA RAZÓN O LA FUERZA

PASAPORTE
PASSPORT

Argentina
Argentine Republic

★ Buenos Aires
🏛 Federal presidential constitutional republic

👥 43,420,000
⌂ 2,780,400 km²
👪 16
GNI 12,460 $
GDP 583.2 bn $
L Spanish
↑ 16 / 142

Extended lowland plains (Pampas), sparsely populated in the south, every third inhabitant lives in the metropolitan region of Buenos Aires. Typical immigration country with numerous minorities of foreign descent (Italians, Germans, etc.) and language enclaves, lots of cattle farming.

Uruguay
Oriental Republic of Uruguay

★ Montevideo
🏛 Unitary parliamentary constitutional republic

👥 3,430,000
⬭ 176,200 km²
👪 19
GNI 15,720 $
GDP 53.4 bn $
L Spanish
↑ 25 / 129

The capital Montevideo is situated a good two hours by ship—via the Rio de la Plata—opposite Buenos Aires. Uruguay is considered Latin America's most European country, first- and second-place soccer World Cup champions; parts of the Pampa grazing land for cattle.

Eur

ope

Iceland
Republic of Iceland

★ Reykjavik

🏛 Unitary parliamentary republic

👥 330,000

⬠ 103,000 km²

👪 3

GNI 50,140 $

GDP 16.6 bn $

L Icelandic

↑ 7/154

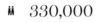

"Land of fire and ice" in the North Atlantic, naturally heated water for everyone. Sparsely populated, about the same number of inhabitants as Malta, but the main island is the largest volcanic island in the world.

Norway
Kingdom of Norway

★ Oslo

🏛 Unitary parliamentary constitutional monarchy

👥 5,200,000

◻ 323,800 km²

👪 16

GNI 93,740 $

GDP 386.6 bn $

L Norwegian

↑ 3 / 158

Breathtaking fjords, carved deeply into the rockbound coast, and vast forests, sparsely populated, not a member of the EU, its wealth is the result of offshore oil deposits. Highly congenial people, including the royal family. Very expensive.

NORGE NOREG
NORWAY

PASS
PASSPORT

Sweden
Kingdom of Sweden

★ Stockholm

🏛 Unitary parliamentary constitutional monarchy

👥 9,800,000

⬜ 450,000 km²

👥 22

GNI 57,920 $

GDP 495.6 bn $

L Swedish

↑ 2 / 159

Social democratic land of longing with high taxes, but for which its citizens get a great deal in return—for instance education or healthcare. Traditional "consensus society" that also takes the democratic minority into account. In the EU but not in the Eurozone.

EUROPEISKA UNIONEN
SVERIGE
PASS

Finland
Republic of Finland

★ Helsinki

🏛 Unitary parlamentary republic

👥 5,480,000

◻ 338,400 km²

👪 16

GNI 46,550 $

GDP 232 bn $

L Finish, Swedish

↑ 3 / 158

Forests, lakes, and saunas. Like Sweden and Norway, sparsely populated. Even more so. Enthusiastic about ice hockey and all winter sports; Finish and Hungarian belong to the same family of languages.

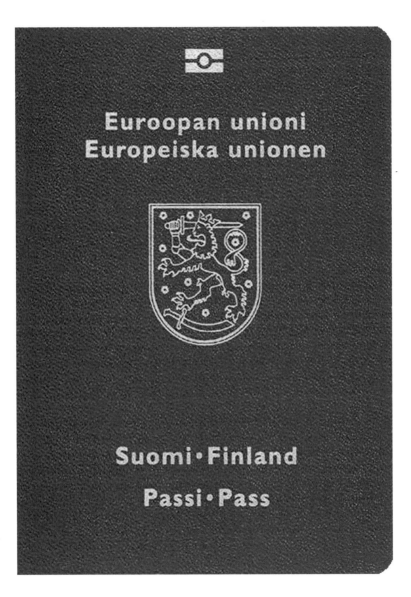

Ireland
Republic of Ireland

★ Dublin
🏛 Unitary parliamentary republic

👫 4,640,000
⬓ 70,300 km²
👪 66
GNI 52,580 $
GDP 283.7 bn $
L English, Irish
↑ 5 / 156

The "green" island with sheep pastures and stone walls is home to triple distilled Irish whiskey and Guinness beer. Once a destitute emigrant nation, deeply Catholic and always with a song in its heart, the EU twice temporarily brought the "Celtic Tiger" to the top of Europe's list of member nations with the highest growth and the lowest unemployment rate.

An tAontas Eorpach
European Union

ÉIRE
IRELAND

Pas
Passport

United Kingdom

United Kingdom of Great Britain and Northern Ireland

★ London

🏛 Unitary parliamentary constitutional monarchy

👥 65,140,000

⌂ 242,900 km²

👪 268

GNI 43,390 $

GDP 2,858 bn $

L English

↑ 3/158

Remainder of the former world empire; England, Scotland, Wales, and Northern Ireland are governed from London, the most posh city on earth; the Queen is the symbolic head of the country's own Anglican church as well as the Commonwealth of Nations.

Denmark
Kingdom of Denmark

★ Copenhagen
🏛 Unitary parliamentary constitutional monarchy

👥 5,680,000
▱ 43,100 km²
👪 132
GNI 58,550 $
GDP 295.1 bn $
L Danish
↑ 3 / 158

Along with Sweden or Norway, alternately occupies the top position in surveys on the sense of communal happiness; the capital Copenhagen is considered one of the most beautiful in Europe. That tiny country bordering Germany that governs giant Greenland.

DEN EUROPÆISKE UNION
DANMARK

PAS

France
French Republic

★ Paris
🏛 Unitary semi-presidential republic

👥 66,810,000
◻ 544,000 km²
👪 123
GNI 40,540 $
GDP 2,418.8 bn $
L French
↑ 3 / 158

The "Grande Nation" that from 1789 onwards guillotined nobles. Still the leading wine-producing country in the world that has everything to offer—from glacial ice to palm-lined beaches; inflicted twice with war by Germany, now Berlin's most important EU partner.

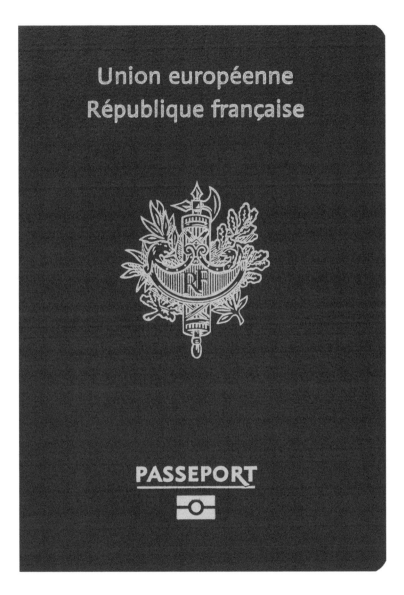

Belgium
Kingdom of Belgium

★ Brussles

🏛 Federal parliamentary constitutional monarchy

👥 11,290,000

⬠ 30,500 km²

⛪ 370

GNI 44,250 $

GDP 455.1 bn $

L German, French, Dutch

↑ 4 / 157

Divided between the Flemings and the Walloons, who warily eye each other. The royal family attempts to unite them. The capital of Brussels is also the headquarters of the EU and NATO. People eat better here than in France. Not only the Belgians say so.

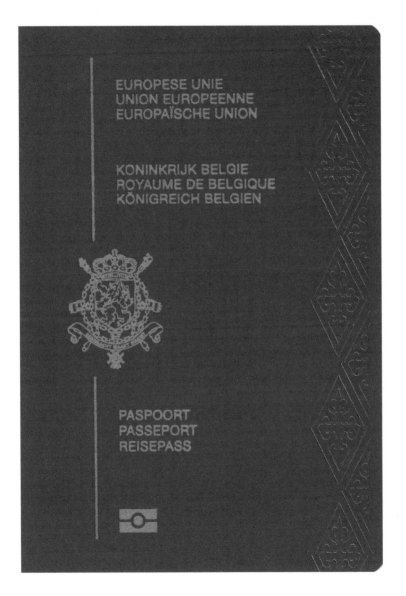

Netherlands
Kingdom of the Netherlands

★ Amsterdam

🏛 Democratic parliamentary constitutional monarchy

👥 16,940,000

◻ 41,526 km²

👥 408

GNI 48,860 $

GDP 750.3 bn $

L Dutch, West Frisian (regionally)

↑ 4 / 157

Country partially wrested from the sea by means of dikes; Schiphol, Amsterdam's airport, lies below sea level. Formerly the cradle of the tolerant society, but nationalistic politicians have also recently become popular. Big history.

EUROPESE UNIE

KONINKRIJK DER NEDERLANDEN

PASPOORT

JE MAINTIENDRAI

Luxembourg
Grand Duchy of Luxembourg

★ Luxembourg City

🏛 Unitary parliamentary constitutional monarchy

👥 570,000

▱ 2,590 km²

👥 220

GNI 77,000 $

GDP 57.8 bn $

L German, French, Luxembourgish

↑ 4/157

The last grand duchy in Europe (Liechtenstein is a principality!); the House of Luxembourg-Nassau appoints the duke, parliamentary democracy; second-smallest EU country after Malta, more important economically than many larger EU countries.

123

Germany
Federal Republic of Germany

★ Berlin

🏛 Federal parliamentary republic

👥 81,410,000

🗌 357,400 km²

👪 228

GNI 45,940 $

GDP 3,363.5 bn $

L German

↑ 1/160

After the Hitler dictatorship, divided for 45 years into West
(pro-America) and East (pro-Moscow), front-line state of the
"Cold War." Now leading economic power in the EU, regular
foreign trade surpluses, now has a fairly good reputation in the
world.

EUROPÄISCHE UNION

BUNDESREPUBLIK
DEUTSCHLAND

REISEPASS

Poland
Republic of Poland

★ Warsaw

🏛 Unitary parliamentary republic

👥 38,000,000

⬭ 312,700 km²

👫 122

GNI 13,340 $

GDP 477.1 bn $

L Polish

↑ 10 / 151

Often did not appear on the map in earlier centuries, in the 20th century crushed between the Soviet Union and Hitler's Germany, has always been oriented toward Western and Central Europe and devoutly Catholic.

Lithuania
Republic of Lithuania

★ Vilnius

🏛 Unitary semi-presidential republic

👫 2,910,000

◻ 65,300 km²

👪 45

GNI 14,940 $

GDP 41.2 bn $

L Lithuanian

↑ 11 / 150

Moderately cool climate with cold winters and moderately warm summers, Baltic Sea remains for the most part free of ice. Population decreasing visibly, favourite destination for emigrants: GB. National sport is basketball, Lithuania's national team are triple European champions.

EUROPOS SĄJUNGA
LIETUVOS RESPUBLIKA

PASAS

Latvia
Republic of Latvia

★ Riga

🏛 Unitary parliamentary constitutional republic

👥 1,980,000

▱ 64,600 km²

👥 31

GNI 14,980 $

GDP 27 bn $

L Latvian

↑ 11 / 150

One of the three states on the Baltic Sea, Riga at the same time the largest Baltic capital; formerly a Soviet republic, today member of the EU and parliamentary democracy. Four national parks, evidence of a European brown bear population of twelve.

Estonia
Republic of Estonia

★ Tallinn
🏛 Parlamentary republic

👫 1,310,000
⬭ 45,300 km²
👪 29
GNI 18,360 $
GDP 22.5 bn $
L Estonian
↑ 12 / 149

The national territory includes 2,000 islands, and forests
cover nearly half of the country. Like all of the Baltic states,
member of the EU since 2004. Formerly Soviet republics
oppressed by Russian immigration, today the Baltic states
fear Russian expansion.

Belarus
Republic of Belarus

★ Minsk

🏛 Unitary presidentialconstitutional republic

👥 9,510,000

⬜ 207,600 km²

👪 46

GNI 6,460 $

GDP 54.6 bn $

L Belarusian, Russian

↑ 58 / 68

Since independence from the USSR dictatorship headed by Alexander Lukashenko. National animal: wisent; close ties to Venezuela since the socialist Chavez regime came to power there with respect to oil, gas.

РЭСПУБЛІКА БЕЛАРУСЬ
РЕСПУБЛИКА БЕЛАРУСЬ
REPUBLIC OF BELARUS

ПАШПАРТ
ПАСПОРТ
PASSPORT

Czech Republic

- ★ Prague
- 🏛 Unitary parliamentary constitutional republic

- 👥 10,550,000
- ⬜ 78,900 km²
- 👥 134
- GNI 18,140 $
- GDP 185.2 bn $
- L Czech
- ↑ 8 / 153

The best beer is brewed here, and per capita consumption is the highest worldwide; the communist government led by Moscow's minions was perceived as a continuation of the occupation by Nazi Germany; the vast majority of the population is not affiliated with any religion.

Slovakia
Slovak Republic

★ Bratislava
🏛 Parliamentary republic

ii 5,420,000
◻ 49,000 km²
👪 111
GNI 17,570 $
GDP 87.2 bn $
L Slovak
↑ 11 / 150

Independent since the peaceful separation from Czechia in
1993. Many "Western" car manufacturers have their automo-
biles produced here. The capital, Bratislava, is situated in the
"Little Carpathians," a good hour away from Vienna by ship
down the Danube.

EURÓPSKA ÚNIA

SLOVENSKÁ REPUBLIKA

CESTOVNÝ PAS

Ukraine

★ Kiew
🏛 Unitary semi-presidential republic

👫 45,200,000
◻ 603,700 km²
👪 75
GNI 2,640 $
GDP 90.6 bn $
L Ukrainian
↑ 49 / 85

Once the "breadbasket" of the Soviet Union, in the Middle Ages Kyiv was the centre of an important dominion, independent since 1991. Conflict with Moscow over the Black Sea peninsula Crimea and parts of eastern Ukraine; Europe's last virgin forests are located in the Ukrainian Carpathians.

Switzerland
Swiss Confederation

★ Bern

🏛 Federal semi-direct democracy under multi-party parliamentary directorial republic

👥 8,290,000

◻ 41,300 km²

👪 201

GNI 84,630 $

GDP 670.8 bn $

L German, French, Italian, Romansh

↑ 4 / 157

Non-EU enclave in Europe and the keeper of many bank secrets, confederation in the idyllic Alps, quadrilingual yet united in maintaining the status quo, famous for cheese, chocolate, and expensive high-end watches.

Schweizer Pass
Passeport suisse
Passaporto svizzero
Passaport svizzer
Swiss passport

Liechtenstein
Principality of Liechtenstein

★ Vaduz

🏛 Unitary parliamentary constitutional monarchy

👥 40,000

⬠ 160 km²

👪 250

GNI 115,530 $ (2009)

GDP 6.7 bn $ (2014)

L German

↑ 12 / 149

Principality with a long tradition in the financial economy, princely family considered one of the wealthiest noble houses in the world, sixth-smallest country on the earth between Switzerland and Austria; "hereditary constitutional monarchy on a democratic basis."

FÜRSTENTUM LIECHTENSTEIN

REISEPASS

Austria
Republic of Austria

★ Vienna
🏛 Federal parliamentary republic

👥 8,610,000
◻ 83,900 km²
👪 103
GNI 47,410 $
GDP 377 bn $
ʟ German
↑ 4 / 157

Alpine and Danube republic comprising remnants of the Habsburg empire; nation of skiers and deeply rooted enthusiasm for music; important tourism sector from Lake Constance in the west to Vienna in the east; excellent cuisine.

EUROPÄISCHE UNION

REPUBLIK ÖSTERREICH

REISEPASS

PASSPORT

Hungary

★ Budapest
🏛 Unitary parlamentary constitutional republic

👫 9,840,000
⌐ 93,000 km²
👪 106
GNI 12,980 $
GDP 121.7 bn $
L Hungarian
↑ 9/152

Opened the "Iron Curtain," vast steppe (puszta), ridiculously difficult language, vacation in the Danube bend or Lake Balaton; the capital of Budapest was the second metropolis of the Austro-Hungarian monarchy, EU member currently with strong nationalist tendencies.

EURÓPAI UNIÓ
MAGYARORSZÁG

ÚTLEVÉL

Romania

★ Bucharest
🏛 Unitary semi-presidential republic

👫 19,830,000
⬜ 238,400 km²
👪 83
GNI 9,500 $
GDP 178 bn $
L Romanian
↑ 15 / 144

Alongside Bulgaria the youngest EU accession country; the communist dictator Ceausescu was Europe's last martinet; very slow economic recovery after his planned economy and the exploitation by his junta.

ROMANIA

PASAPORT

Moldova
Republic of Moldova

★ Chisinau
🏛 Unitary parliamentary republic

👪 3,550,000
⬭ 33,800 km²
👪 105
GNI 2,240 $
GDP 6.6 bn $
L Romanian
↑ 43 / 104

Surrounded on three sides by Ukrainian territory, therefore
no Black Sea coast; majority of the population Romanian;
supported by the USA, extensive free trade with the inner-
European market; agricultural products: wine, spirits, and
preserved food.

REPUBLICA MOLDOVA

PAȘAPORT

Portugal
Portuguese Republic

★ Lisbon

🏛 Unitary semi-presidential constitutional republic

👥 10,350,000

◠ 92,300 km²

👥 112

GNI 20,530 $

GDP 198.9 bn $

L Portuguese

↑ 4/157

Numerous discoverers embarked from here for the New World; also became a democracy concurrent with the end of the dictatorship in Spain in the second half of the 20th century; the Atlantic coast attracts vacationers en masse; the capital Lisbon is lovely.

UNIÃO EUROPEIA
PORTUGAL
PASSAPORTE

Spain
Kingdom of Spain

★ Madrid

🏛 Unitary parliamentary constitutional monarchy

👥 46,420,000

⬠ 505,000 km²

👪 92

GNI 28,530 $

GDP 1,199.1 bn $

L Spanish,
Basque (regionally),
Catalan (regionally),
Galician (regionally)

↑ 3 / 158

Traces of Moorish occupation until the late 15th century are visible to this day in the south; former world power. Did not become democratic in the 20th century until the end of the Franco dictatorship in 1977, member of the EU; sunny vacation country; important cultural treasures.

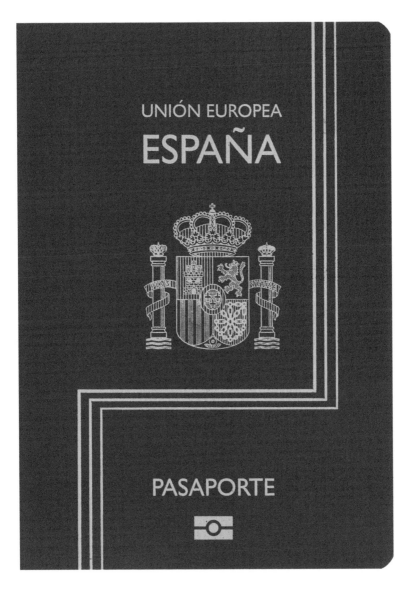

UNIÓN EUROPEA
ESPAÑA

PASAPORTE

Andorra
Principality of Andorra

★ Andorra la Vella

🏛 Unitary parliamentary
   Semi-Elective diarchy

👥 70,000

⬭ 470 km²

👪 149

GNI 43,270 $ (2013)

GDP 3.2 bn $ (2013)

L Spanish, French,
   Portugese

↑ 18 / 140

Miniature state in the eastern Pyrenees between Spain and
France, tax haven; major revenue source: winter sports
tourism. Only country with two foreigners as head of state:
France's president and the Bishop of Urgell.

ANDORRA

PASSAPORT

Monaco
Principality of Monaco

★ Monaco
🏛 Unitary parliamentary constitutional monarchy

👥 40,000
🗍 2 km²
🏛 20,000
GNI 186,710 $ (2008)
GDP 6.1 bn $ (2011)
L French
↑ 14 / 145

Tiny but rich Monégasque monarchy thanks to tax breaks for high society and a famous gambling casino, the annual Formula 1 auto race, and the demurrages in the yacht harbour.

Italy
Italian Republic

★ Rome
🏛 Unitary parliamentary republic

👥 60,800,000
◻ 301,300 km²
👥 202
GNI 32,810 $
GDP 1,821.5 bn $
L Italian,
   German (regional),
   French (regional),
   Slovenian (regional)
↑ 3 / 158

Wonder chamber of art history, masses of tourist attractions, memorable boot-shaped outline in the Mediterranean; democratic-chaotic form of government and constantly on the verge of national bankruptcy; home of the "bella figura."

UNIONE EUROPEA

REPUBBLICA ITALIANA

PASSAPORTO

San Marino
Republic of San Marino

★ San Marino
🏛 Unitary parliamentary directorial republic

👥 30,000
⬜ 61 km²
👥 492
GNI 52,140 $ (2008)
GDP 1.9 bn $ (2008)
L Italian
↑ 17 / 141

Miniature state, easy to overlook, roughly between Bologna and Rimini; entirely surrounded by Italy; but the oldest existing republic in the world. Supposedly founded in 301 CE by Saint Marinus, not in the EU. Shares the nickname "La Serenissima" with Venice.

REPUBBLICA DI SAN MARINO
RÉPUBLIQUE DE SAINT-MARIN
REPUBLIC OF SAN MARINO

PASSAPORTO
PASSEPORT
PASSPORT

Vatican City

★ Vatican City State

🏛 Absolute monarchy, exxlestiastical and elective theocracy

👫 0.001

⬜ 0.44 km²

👪 2,273

GNI n.d.

GDP n.d.

L German, Italian, Latin

↑ 22 / 132

As the "Holy See" the object of international law, with the head of the Roman-Catholic Church, the Pope, the chief of state who governs with absolute power, situated in downtown Rome, smallest nation in the world.

Slovenia
Republic of Slovenia

★ Ljubljana
🏛 Unitary parliamentary constitutional
republic

👫 2,060,000
⬜ 20,300 km²
👪 101
GNI 22,190 $
GDP 42.8 bn $
L Slovene
↑ 11 / 150

Idyllic alpine, lake, and hiking landscape, a total of 10,000 km
of hiking trails, northern Balkan peninsula with access to the
Adriatic Sea from the small port in Piran; the capital Ljubljana
offers well-preserved, distinct Art Nouveau architecture.

EVROPSKA UNIJA
REPUBLIKA SLOVENIJA

POTNI LIST

Croatia
Republic of Croatia

★ Zagreb

🏛 Unitary parliamentary constitutional republic

👥 4,220,000

◻ 56,500 km²

👥 75

GNI 12,700 $

GDP 48.7 bn $

L Croatian

↑ 15 / 144

Catholic part of former Yugoslavia, hence age old hostility with the orthodox Serbs, which led to the war after the collapse of Yugoslavia; today popular vacation destination with a wonderful island world in the Adriatic Sea.

REPUBLIKA HRVATSKA
REPUBLIC OF CROATIA
RÉPUBLIQUE DE CROATIE

PUTOVNICA
PASSPORT
PASSEPORT

Bosnia and Herzegovina

★ Sarajevo

🏛 Federal parliamentary republic

👥 3,810,000

⬭ 51,100 km²

👪 75

GNI 4,670 $

GDP 16.2 bn $

L Bosnian, Croatian, Serbian

↑ 45 / 102

Here, the Muslim Bosniaks (50.7 % of the population) and the Catholic Croatians (15.2 %) use letters from the Latin alphabet, the Orthodox Serbians (30.7 %) use Cyrillic letters. They do not share any holidays; the state presidency consists of one representative from each group.

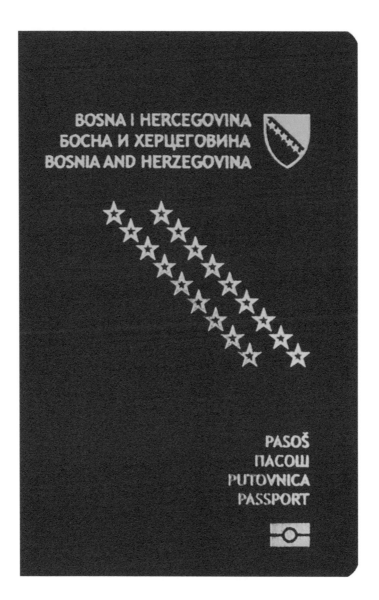

Serbia
Republic of Serbia

★ Belgrade
🏛 Unitary parliamentary constitutional republic

👥 7,100,000
⬜ 77,500 km²
👪 92
GNI 5,540 $
GDP 37.1 bn $
L Serbian
↑ 37 / 112

Largest individual state of what was formerly Yugoslavia; in the 1990s the army, dominated by Serbs, waged a war against other individual states that had declared independence. Serbian Orthodox; traditional ties with Moscow; rich cultural history.

Montenegro

★ Podgorica
🏛 Parliamentary republic

👫 620,000
⬜ 13,800 km²
👨‍👩‍👧 45
GNI 7,220 $
GDP 4 bn $
L Montenegrin
↑ 43 / 104

After the Balkan Wars in the 1990s formed a loose confederation with Serbia. Independent since 2006, like Serbia predominately Serbian Orthodox; more than 20 % of the GDP
from tourism; biggest human rights problem: organised crime.

CRNA GORA
MONTENEGRO

PASOŠ
PASSPORT
PASSEPORT

Kosovo
Republic of Kosovo

★ Priština
🏛 Unitary Parliamentary republic

👥 1,800,000
⬠ 10,900 km²
👥 165
GNI 3,970 $
GDP 6.4 bn $
L Albanian, Serbian
↑ 85 / 41

Most states in the UN recognise Kosovo as independent (since 2008); formerly part of Yugoslavia, then Serbia; energy problems, exports: iron, steel, and ore; according to the USA important drug route from Afghanistan to Western Europe.

REPUBLIKA E KOSOVËS
РЕПУБЛИКА КОСОВО
REPUBLIC OF KOSOVO

PASAPORTË
ПАСОШ
PASSPORT

Bulgaria
Republic of Bulgaria

★ Sofia
🏛 Unitary parliamentary republic

👥 7,180,000
⌂ 111,000 km²
👨‍👩‍👧 65
GNI 7,480 $
GDP 50.2 bn $
L Bulgarian
↑ 15 / 144

With Romania youngest member of the EU; national language Bulgarian in Cyrillic letters, large Turkish minority with its own dialect that strongly differs from Turkish. The landscape has everything to offer—from the alpine Balkan Mountains to the shores of the Black Sea.

ЕВРОПЕЙСКИ СЪЮЗ
EUROPEAN UNION

РЕПУБЛИКА БЪЛГАРИЯ
REPUBLIC OF BULGARIA

ПАСПОРТ
PASSPORT

Albania
Republic Albanien

★ Tirana

🏛 Unitary parliamentary constitutional
republic

👥 2,980,000

⌂ 28,800 km²

👪 103

GNI 4,280 $

GDP 11.4 bn $

L Albanian

↑ 47/97

Isolated for decades after banishing the king, even within the
"Eastern bloc" itself. Dictator Hoxhat turned to Beijing. Barren
mountainous country, in parts blood feuds; pastoral people;
in the early 1990s two phases of mass flight via the Adriatic
Sea to Italy.

REPUBLIKA E SHQIPËRISË
REPUBLIC OF ALBANIA

PASAPORTË
PASSPORT

Macedonia
Republic of Macedonia

★ Skopje
🏛 Parliamentary republic

👥 2,080,000
◻ 25,700 km²
👥 81
GNI 5,140 $
GDP 10.1 bn $
L Albanian,
    Macedonian
↑ 41 / 107

Because of the region in Greece of the same name, also called the Former Yugoslavian Republic of Macedonia; independent since 1991, historically embattled and occupied by foreigners, politically "mixed up," hence the Italian and French words for fruit salad.

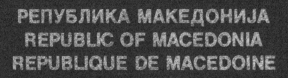

РЕПУБЛИКА МАКЕДОНИЈА
REPUBLIC OF MACEDONIA
REPUBLIQUE DE MACEDOINE

ПАСОШ
PASSPORT
PASSEPORT

Greece
Hellenic Republic

★ Athens

🏛 Unitary presidential constitutional republic

👥 10,820,000

◻ 132,000 km²

👪 82

GNI 20,320 $

GDP 194.9 bn $

L Greek

↑ 6 / 155

The cradle of occidental thought (politics, philosophy, the natural sciences), occupied by Turks for more than 400 years. Today a vacation destination with numerous islands in the Mediterranean, ancient excavation sites, EU member with financial problems.

ΕΥΡΩΠΑΪΚΗ ΕΝΩΣΗ
ΕΛΛΗΝΙΚΗ ΔΗΜΟΚΡΑΤΙΑ

ΔΙΑΒΑΤΗΡΙΟ

Malta
Republic of Malta

★ Valletta
🏛 Unitary parliamentary republic

ⅈ 430,000
⬜ 320 km²
🏢 1,344
GNI 23,930 $
GDP 9.7 bn $
ʟ English, Maltese
↑ 8 / 153

More Catholic churches per capita than Rome, treeless Mediterranean island, lingua francas: Maltese, English, and Italian; Maltese is the only Semitic language in Latin letters, about the same size as Munich.

Turkey
Republic of Turkey

★ Ankara

🏛 Unitary parliamentary constitutional republic

👥 78,670,000

⬜ 783,600 km²

⛪ 100

GNI 9,950 $

GDP 717.9 bn $

L Turkish

↑ 43 / 104

Remainder of the Ottoman Empire, secularized in the 20th century by Atatürk, the country's founder, whose legacy was guarded by a strong military; massive labor migration to Western Europe, especially Germany, meanwhile governed almost autocratically by a strong, religiously oriented movement.

TÜRKİYE CUMHURİYETİ
REPUBLIC OF TURKEY

PASAPORT
PASSPORT

Cyprus
Republic of Cyprus

★ Nicosia

🏛 Unitary presidential constitutional republic

👤 1,170,000

⬠ 5,400 km²

👥 217

GNI 25,990 $

GDP 19.6 bn $

L Greek, Turkish

↑ 13 / 148

Mediterranean island, the third largest after Sicily and Sardinia, contested by Turkey and Greece and divided into north and south since 1974. UN forces protect a "buffer zone" that separates the island and the capital of Nicosia, about one million inhabitants.

ΕΥΡΩΠΑΪΚΗ ΕΝΩΣΗ
AVRUPA BİRLİĞİ
EUROPEAN UNION

ΚΥΠΡΙΑΚΗ ΔΗΜΟΚΡΑΤΙΑ
KIBRIS CUMHURİYETİ
REPUBLIC OF CYPRUS

ΔΙΑΒΑΤΗΡΙΟ
PASAPORT
PASSPORT

Georgia

★ Tiflis

🏛 Unitary semi-presidential
constitutional republic

👥 3,680,000

⬜ 69,700 km²

⛩ 53

GNI 4,160 $

GDP 14 bn $

L Georgian

↑ 44 / 103

Former Soviet republic, native country of Stalin, whom some
Georgians still venerate. Between Europe and Asia, Caucasus
Mountains keep cold air from blowing in from the north and
the Black Sea warm. Regions of Abkhazia and South-East
Ossetia separatist, their independence recognised almost
solely by Moscow.

Armenia
Republic of Armenien

★ Yerevan
🏛 Unitary semi-presidential republic

👥 3,020,000
🔲 29,700 km²
👥 102
GNI 3,880$
GDP 10.5 bn $
L Armenian
↑ 67/59

Caucasian mountainous country between Azerbaijan, Georgia, Turkey, and Iran; Armenian Apostolic Church among 94% of the population. The settlement area of the Armenians (since 2,700 BCE) was once much larger, systematic genocide by the Turks in the early 20th century.

196

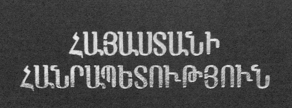

ՀԱՅԱՍՏԱՆԻ
ՀԱՆՐԱՊԵՏՈՒԹՅՈՒՆ

ԱՆՁՆԱԳԻՐ

REPUBLIC OF ARMENIA
PASSPORT

Azerbaijan
Republic of Azerbaijan

★ Baku
🏛 Unitary dominant-partysemi-presidential republic

👥 9,650,000
⬜ 86,600 km²
👫 111
GNI 6,560 $
GDP 53.1 bn $
L Azerbaijani
↑ 63 / 63

Nearly 10 million inhabitants, Muslim, ongoing dispute with Armenia over Nagorno-Karabakh. Promotes its interests with "caviar" diplomacy (invitation, gifts, money) among representatives of the European Council and the Bundestag; Baku calls the reports "fake news from Armenia."

AZƏRBAYCAN RESPUBLİKASI
REPUBLIC OF AZERBAIJAN

PASPORT
PASSPORT

Russia
Russian Federation

★ Moscow
🏛 Federal semi-presidential
constitutional republic

👥 144,100,000
◰ 17,098,200 km²
👪 8
GNI 11,450 $
GDP 1,331.2 bn $
L Russian
↑ 42 / 105

Largest country in the world, as big as Europe and Australia together, seven time zones, before 1989 as the USSR the USA's countervailing force in the "Cold War," Wild West capitalism since, vast occurrences of natural resources and energy sources; world power of chess.

РОССИЙСКАЯ ФЕДЕРАЦИЯ
RUSSIAN FEDERATION

ПАСПОРТ
PASSPORT

Afr

ica

Morocco
Kingdom of Morocco

★ Rabat
🏛 Unitary parliamentary constitutional monarchy

👥 34,380,000
⌂ 458,800 km²
👪 75
GNI 3,030 $
GDP 100.6 bn $
L Arabic
↑ 71/55

Constitutional monarchy since 1992, the most Western Maghreb state, since the 1990s transit country for people from sub-Saharan Africa. Itself a classic emigrant country; Moroccans often constitute the largest Muslim community in their host country, high birth rate.

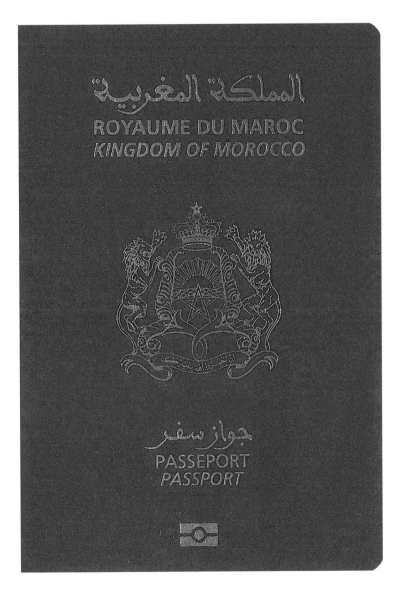

Algeria
People's Democratic Republic
of Algeria

★ Algiers

🏛 Unitary semi-presidentialpeople's republic

👥 39,670,000

◻ 2,381,700 km²

👥 17

GNI 4,870 $

GDP 166.8 bn $

L Arabic, Berber

↑ 78 / 48

After the division of Sudan Africa's largest territorial state, like Morocco parts of the Atlas Mountains, extremely dry desert climate in the sparsely populated south, Mediterranean climate in the north; democracy only feigned; Islamic rebels, long-standing civil war.

الجمهورية الجزائرية الديمقراطية الشعبية

REPUBLIQUE ALGERIENNE
DEMOCRATIQUE ET POPULAIRE
PEOPLE'S DEMOCRATIC
REPUBLIC OF ALGERIA

جواز السفر

PASSEPORT
PASSPORT

Tunisia
Republic of Tunisia

★ Tunis
🏛 Unitary semi-presidental constitutional republic

👤 11,110,000
⬜ 163,600 km²
👥 68
GNI 3,980 $
GDP 43 bn $
L Arabic
↑ 64 / 62

Maghreb state between Libya and Algeria with Mediterranean shoreline fully developed for tourists, especially the offshore island of Djerba. Agriculturally strong, among the leading producers of olive oil, lowest birth rate in the Arab world.

REPUBLIQUE TUNISIENNE
REPUBLIC OF TUNISIA

PASSEPORT
PASSPORT

Libya

★ Tripoli
🏛 Provisional government

👥 6,280,000
⬭ 1,775,500 km²
👪 4
GNI 4,660 $(2011)
GDP 34.7 bn $ (2011)
ʟ Arabic
↑ 88 / 37

Once an Italian colony, then kingdom, replaced in 1969 by a bloodless putsch by "revolutionary leader" Gaddafi; governed until 2011 (!). Pension system financed by oil revenue; long-term political goal: pan-Arab unification; rebels toppled Gaddafi regime in 2011, civil war with foreign participation since.

Egypt
Arab Republic of Egypt

★ Cairo

🏛 Unitary semi-presidential republic

👫 91,510,000

🗌 1,001,500 km²

👪 91

GNI 3,340 $

GDP 330.8 bn $

L Arabic

↑ 75 / 51

One of the earliest high cultures, fertile along the banks of the Nile. Former head of state Nasser dreams of Pan-Arabia and the annihilation of Israel; first peace agreement with Israel under Sadat, his successor Mubarak was toppled during the "Arab Spring."

جمهورية مصر العربية

ARAB REPUBLIC OF EGYPT

جواز سفر

PASSPORT

213

Mauritania
Islamic Republic of Mauritania

★ Nouakchott

🏛 Unitary semi-presidential republic

👥 4,070,000

⬜ 1,030,700 km²

👪 4

GNI 1,370 $ (2014)

GDP 5.4 bn $ (2014)

L Arabic

↑ 73/53

In the mid-20th century 90% of the population still lived as
nomads in tents; larger cities developed only later, where
today about half of the country's citizens live; Arabian, Berber,
and sub-Saharan shares of the population; slavery continues
to exist.

الجمهورية الإسلامية الموريتانية

REPUBLIQUE ISLAMIQUE
DE MAURITANIE
ISLAMIC REPUBLIC
OF MAURITANIA

جواز

PASSEPORT
PASSPORT

Mali
Republic of Mali

★ Bamako
🏛 Unitary semi-presidential republic

👥 17,600,000
◻ 1,240,200 km²
👥 14
GNI 760 $
GDP 12.8 bn $
L French
↑ 75 / 51

Half of the population below poverty level, once the cultural bloom of three Islamic empires; today conflict between separatist Tuareg and the army in the north, furthermore fighting with Islamists; agriculture, fishing mining, exports: gold, salt.

REPUBLIQUE DU MALI

PASSEPORT

Niger
Republic of Niger

★ Niamey
🏛 Unitary semi-presidential republic

👥 19,900,000
⬜ 1,267,000 km²
👪 16
GNI 390 $
GDP 7.1 bn $
L French
↑ 75 / 51

Deserts traversed by the Niger River; highest fertility rate in the world, most important export: uranium. USA under G.W. Bush wanted to prove that Niger supplied Iraq with weapon-grade uranium, smuggled the corresponding fake papers into Niger's embassy in Rome.

REPUBLIQUE DU NIGER

PASSEPORT

219

Chad
Republic of Chad

★ N'Djamena
🏛 Dominant-party presidential republic

👥 14,040,000
⬠ 1,284,000 km²
👥 11
GNI 880 $
GDP 10.9 bn $
L Arabic, French
↑ 77/47

Almost 200 ethnic groups, just over 50% of the population Muslim; vast deserts but has one of Africa's largest nature reserves. Attacked by Libya in the early 1990s, liberated by the one-time colonial power of France, since then a republic.

REPUBLIQUE DU TCHAD

جمهورية تشاد

REPUBLIC OF CHAD

PASSEPORT

جواز سفر

PASSPORT

Sudan
Republic of Sudan

★ Khartum

🏛 Dominant-pary federal
   semi-presidential republic

👥 40,230,000

▭ 1,840,700 km²

👥 22

GNI 1,920 $

GDP 97.2 bn $

L Arabic

↑ 88 / 37

Every fifth inhabitant (of a total of nearly 37 million) lives
in or near the capital of Khartoum. The Blue and the White
Nile join up here. Parts of the Sahelian zone, various savannas (from briar savannas in dry regions to wet savannas),
10 national parks.

جمهورية السودان

THE REPUBLIC OF THE SUDAN

جواز سفر

PASSPORT

Eritrea
State of Eritrea

★ Asmara

🏛 Unitary one-party presidential republic

👥 4,800,000

⌂ 121,100 km²

🏛 40

GNI 480 $ (2011)

GDP 2.6 bn $ (2011)

L Arabic, Tigrinya

↑ 86 / 39

An arid savanna climate prevails near the Red Sea (which gives the country its name), rainfall in the mountains and inland. Majority of the population works in the small-scale agricultural sector; further diminished after the border war with Ethiopia; popular sport is bicycle racing (!).

ERITREA

ኤርትራ ارتريا

PASSPORT

ፓስፖርት جواز سفر

225

Djibouti
Republic of Djibouti

- ★ Djibouti City
- 🏛 Dominant-party semi-presidential republic

- 👥 890,000
- ⬡ 23,200 km²
- 👥 38
- **GNI** 1,030 $ (2005)
- **GDP** 1.7 bn $
- **L** Arabic, French
- ↑ 83 / 43

Opposite Yemen over the Red Sea, further borders with Somalia, Eritrea, Ethiopia. Multiform desert landscape, paradise for divers. Independent from France since 1977. Small country with uniform climate, high summer all year by the sea.

Ethiopia
Federal Democratic Republic
of Ethiopia

★ Addis Abeba
🏛 Federal parliamentary republic

👥 99,390,000
⬠ 1,133,400 km²
👪 88
GNI 590 $
GDP 61.5 bn $
L Amharic
↑ 87 / 38

About 3 times as big as Germany, almost 100 million inhabitants, occupied by Italy under Mussolini from 1939 to 1941. Long-standing regent was Haile Selassie, the last "Emperor of Abyssinia," who saw himself as the 225th successor of the biblical King Solomon.

የኢትዮጵያ ፌዴራላዊ
ዲሞክራሲያዊ ሪፐብሊክ

FEDERAL DEMOCRATIC REPUBLIC
OF ETHIOPIA

ፓስፖርት

PASSPORT

Somalia
Federal Republic of Somalia

★ Mogadishu
🏛 Federal parliamentary republic

👥 10,790,000
⬠ 637,700 km²
👥 17
GNI n.d.
GDP 5.9 bn $
L Somali
↑ 89 / 33

Situated on the Somali Peninsula at the Horn of Africa; soil erosion and desert expansion due to overgrazing and deforestation; firewood the only source of energy; civil war. Offshore dumping, in part with nuclear waste, and uncontrolled over-fishing.

Senegal
Republic of Senegal

★ Dakar
🏛 Semi-presidential republic

👥 15,130,000
⬜ 196,700 km²
👥 77
GNI 980 $
GDP 13.6 bn $
L French
↑ 71 / 55

Stretches along the West African coast from the southern edge of the Sahara to the northern edge of the tropical jungle. Independent since 1960, in previous centuries plagued by slavery. Islam is the state religion, the south (Casamance) divided by Gambia.

COMMUNAUTE ECONOMIQUE DES
ETATS DE L'AFRIQUE DE L'OUEST

REPUBLIQUE DU SENEGAL

PASSEPORT
Passport

Gambia
Islamic Republic of Gambia

★ Banjul
🏛 Unitary presidential republic

👥 1,990,000
⬜ 11,300 km²
👪 176
GNI 460 $ (2014)
GDP 0.9 bn $
L English
↑ 61 / 65

Except for a section on the west coast of Africa, completely surrounded by Senegal; smallest state in continental Africa on both sides of the Gambia River. Big game already exterminated by colonial rulers, still has an abundant world of fauna and flora.

Guinea-Bissau
Republic of Guinea-Bissau

★ Bissau

🏛 Unitary semi-presidential republic

👥 1,840,000

⬜ 36,100 km²

👥 51

GNI 590 $

GDP 1.1 bn $

L Portuguese

↑ 77/47

One of the worst developed countries in the world, population of ca. 1.5 million, 7 doctors per 100,000 inhabitants; genital mutilation among women still widespread. According to the UN hub of drug trade; 85% of the exports are cashews (!).

REPÚBLICA DA GUINÉ-BISSAU
REPUBLIQUE DE GUINÉE-BISSAU
REPUBLIC OF GUINEA-BISSAU

PASSAPORTE
PASSEPORT
PASSPORT

Guinea
Republic of Guinea

★ Conakry
🏛 Presidential republic

👫 12,610,000
⬭ 245,900 km²
👪 51
GNI 470 $
GDP 6.7 bn $
L French
↑ 71/55

Military dictatorship since its foundation in 1958, constitution is almost never implemented; the German Bundeswehr also trains/trained soldiers; rivers Niger and Gambia have their source here, and it is also one of the headstreams of the Senegal River; rain forest in the high-, grass savannas in the lowlands.

COMMUNAUTÉ ÉCONOMIQUE DES
ÉTATS DE L'AFRIQUE DE L'OUEST
(CEDEAO)

RÉPUBLIQUE DE GUINÉE

PASSEPORT

239

Sierra Leone
Republic of Sierra Leone

★ Freetown

🏛 Unitary parliamentary constitutional republic

👫 6,450,000

⬭ 71,700 km²

👪 90

GNI 620 $

GDP 4.2 bn $

L English

↑ 66 / 60

Decades of war over diamonds and other natural resources. Currently dealing with the past, after slave trade beginning in the 18th century by the British increasingly Islamic, now 70 % Sunni Islam; 70 % of its citizens are "extremely poor" (less than US $1.00 daily).

Liberia
Republic of Liberia

★ Monrovia
🏛 Unitary presidential republic

👥 4,500,000
⬠ 97,800 km²
👪 46
GNI 380 $
GDP 2.1 bn $
L English
↑ 79 / 47

Created during the repatriation of slaves from the USA; independent since 1847. Conflicts between the local population
and repatriates or their descendants since; foreign troops in
the country for internal security; fishing accounts for 15 % of
the GDP.

REPUBLIC OF LIBERIA

PASSPORT
PASSEPORT

Ivory Coast
Republic of Côte d'Ivoire

★ Yamoussoukro

🏛 Unitary presidential republic

👥 22,700,000

◰ 322,500 km²

👥 70

GNI 1,420 $

GDP 31.8 bn $

L French

↑ 71 / 55

Named after elephant tusks (long the most important export), independent since 1960, stable for 40 years; coffee and cocoa export ensured prosperity, decline of the price for cocoa resulted in unrest and civil war, peace agreement in 2007. Dealing with the past continues.

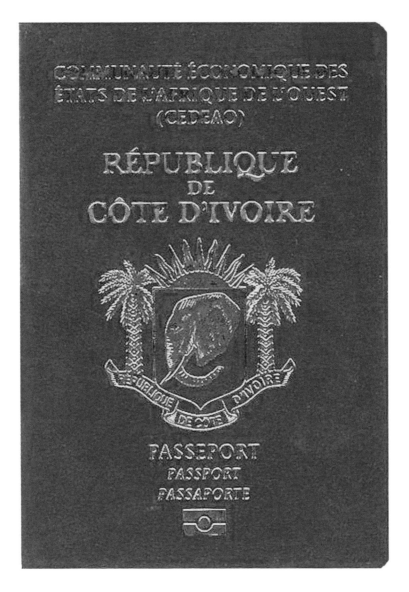

Burkina Faso

★ Ouagadougou
🏛 Unitary semi-presidential republic

👥 18,100,000
⬭ 274,000 km²
👪 66
GNI 640 $
GDP 10.7 bn $
L French
↑ 72 / 54

Name means "land of honest men." Independent since 1960, until 1984 named "Upper Volta"; frequent droughts; 9 out of 10 inhabitants raise crops to meet their personal needs; good cotton does not reach the EU or the USA due to subsidies; however, both pay subsidies.

Ghana
Republic of Ghana

★ Accra

🏛 Unitary presidential constitutional republic

👥 27,410,000

⬭ 238,500 km²

👪 115

GNI 1,480 $

GDP 37.5 bn $

L English

↑ 67 / 59

Pretty much exactly 50 % Christians and 50 % Muslims, almost as big as the United Kingdom, the former colonial power. Second largest cocoa producer worldwide, nearly ⅓ of the exports gold, followed by oil, diamonds, and bauxite.

ECONOMIC COMMUNITY OF
WEST AFRICAN STATES
(ECOWAS)

COMMUNAUTE ECONOMIQUE DES
ETATS DE L'AFRIQUE DE L'OUEST
(CEDEAO)

REPUBLIC OF GHANA

PASSPORT
PASSEPORT

Togo
Republic of Togo

★ Lomé

🏛 Presidential republic

👥 7,300,000

⬭ 56,800 km²

👥 129

GNI 540 $

GDP 4.1 bn $

L Ewe, French, Kabiyé

↑ 74 / 52

1884–16 the "German Colony of Togo," thereafter League of Nations or UN region. Autocratically governed by the father of the current head of state for 40 years, human rights violations; sandy beaches, palms, savannas with antelopes and elephants in the backlands.

COMMUNAUTE ECONOMIQUE DES
ETATS DE L'AFRIQUE DE L'OUEST

(CEDEAO / ECOWAS)

REPUBLIQUE TOGOLAISE

PASSEPORT

Benin
Republic of Benin

★ Porto Novo
🏛 Presidential republic

👪 10,880,000
◠ 112,600 km²
👪 97
GNI 840
GDP 8.3 bn $
L French
↑ 69 / 57

"Dahomey" until 1975, savannas, rain and dry forests; remnant population of big game, over 50 local languages besides the official language of French. 75 % of all women and 60 % of all men over 15 are illiterate; first country in Africa to prohibit the circumcision of young girls.

Communauté Economique
des Etats
de l'Afrique de l'Ouest

REPUBLIQUE DU BENIN

PASSEPORT

Nigeria
Federal Republic of Nigeria

★ Abuja

🏛 Federal presidential republic

👥 182,200,000

⬜ 923,800 km²

👥 197

GNI 2,820 $

GDP 481.1 bn $

L English

↑ 82 / 44

By far the most populous country in Africa, with more than 500 spoken languages (!). Democracy and development slow, corruption prevents profits from oil deposits; conflicts between the Muslim north and the Christian south.

ECONOMIC COMMUNITY OF
WEST AFRICAN STATES
(ECOWAS)

FEDERAL REPUBLIC OF NIGERIA

PASSPORT

Cameroon
Republic of Cameroon

★ Yaoundé

🏛 Unitary dominant-partypresidential
republic

👥 23,340,000

⬭ 475,400 km²

👥 49

GNI 1,320 $

GDP 28.4 bn $

L English, French

↑ 80 / 46

Has nearly all of the types of landscapes and climate zones
on the African continent; a stable majority democracy for
which the order of succession for the governing head of state
is endangered.

COMMUNAUTE ECONOMIQUE ET
MONETAIRE DE L'AFRIQUE CENTRALE

ECONOMIC AND MONETARY
COMMUNITY OF CENTRAL AFRICA

REPUBLIQUE DU CAMEROUN

REPUBLIC OF CAMEROON

PASSEPORT

PASSPORT

Central African Republic

★ Bangui
🏛 Semi-presidential republic

👥 4,900,000
⬜ 622,500 km²
👥 8
GNI 330 $
GDP 1.6 bn $
L French, Sango
↑ 80 / 46

Rainforest in south refuge for lowland gorillas and forest elephants. Birth rate: five children per woman, only 7% of married women have access to birth control; weak healthcare system. Few representatives of the indigenous pygmies in the southwestern rainforest.

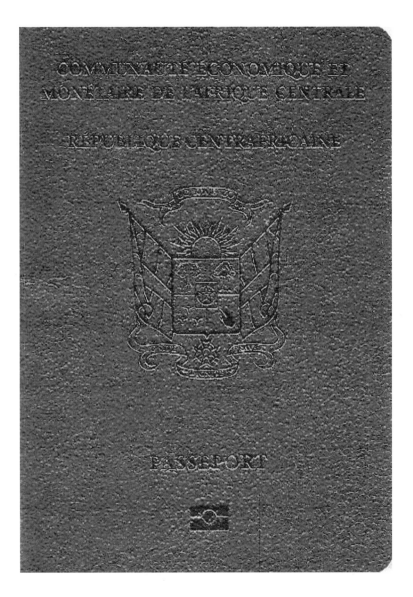

COMMUNAUTÉ ÉCONOMIQUE ET
MONÉTAIRE DE L'AFRIQUE CENTRALE

RÉPUBLIQUE CENTRAFRICAINE

PASSEPORT

South Sudan
Republic of South Sudan

★ Juba
🏛 Federal presidential constitutional republic

👥 12,340,000
⬠ 620,000 km²
👥 20
GNI 790 $
GDP 9 bn $
ʟ English, Arabic
↑ 87/38

Independent from Sudan since 2011; internal civil war between members of various tribes, mass flight, famine in the Darfur region. Peace agreement mediated with international assistance fragile. Child marriage widespread according to AI.

REPUBLIC
OF
SOUTH SUDAN

PASSPORT

Equatorial Guinea
Republic of Equatorial Guinea

★ Malabo
🏛 Dominant party presidential republic

👥 850,000
⬜ 28,000 km²
👨‍👦 30
GNI 12,820 $
GDP 12.2 bn $
L French, Portuguese, Spanish
↑ 80 / 46

State territory either south (islands) or north of the equator, which nowhere traverses the country; sub-Saharan Africa. Major offshore oil deposits, yet profits go to a small clique around political powers that be; no legal security.

REPUBLICA
DE
GUINEA ECUATORIAL

PASAPORTE

Gabon
Gabonese Republic

★ Libreville
🏛 Dominant party presidential republic

👥 1,730,000
⬜ 267,700 km²
👪 6
GNI 9,200 $
GDP 14.3 bn $
L French
↑ 75 / 51

Extremely sparsely populated, area ³/₄ of that in Germany,
population like Hamburg, 40 languages; Albert Schweitzer's
jungle clinic in Lambaréné; wood, textile, and paper industry.
The most well known Gabonese: soccer star Pierre-Emerick
Aubameyang.

REPUBLIQUE
GABONAISE

PASSEPORT
PASSPORT

Republic of Congo

★ Brazzaville
🏛 Presidential republic

👥 4,620,000
⬓ 342,000 km²
👨‍👩‍👧 14
GNI 2,540 $
GDP 8.6 bn $
L French
↑ 81 / 45

Capital of Brazzaville at Pool Malebo (widening of the Congo) opposite Kinshasa, average age of the Congolese: 19.6 yrs., 98 % belong to the Bantu tribe. Christian majority. Tropical rainforest, high malnutrition rate.

COMMUNAUTÉ ÉCONOMIQUE
ET MONÉTAIRE
DE L'AFRIQUE CENTRALE

RÉPUBLIQUE DU CONGO

PASSEPORT

Democratic Republic of Congo

★ Kinshasa
🏛 Unitary semi-presidentialrepublic

👥 77,270,000
◻ 2,344,900 km²
👥 33
GNI 410 $
GDP 35.2 bn $
L French
↑ 84 / 42

1971 to 1997 "Zaire" (terror regime with self-enrichment under dictator Mobutu, once assistant to P. Lumumba, who led the country to independence, murdered with Western help). Capital of Kinshasa at Pool Malebo across from Brazzaville.

République Démocratique du Congo

JUSTICE PAIX TRAVAIL

PASSEPORT

Uganda
Republic of Uganda

★ Kampala

🏛 Dominant-party semi-presidential republic

👥 39,030,000

⬜ 241,600 km²

👥 162

GNI 700 $

GDP 27.5 bn $

L English

↑ 66 / 60

Parts of Lake Victoria; virgin forest, savanna, 40 different ethnic groups with about as many languages. Independent from GB since 1962, then terror regimes under Milton Obote and Idi Amin, extremely severe human rights violations, wars against neighboring states.

Republic of
UGANDA

PASSPORT

271

Kenya
Republic of Kenya

★ Nairobi

🏛 Unitary presidential constitutional republic

👥 46,050,000

◻ 582,600 km²

👪 79

GNI 1,340 $

GDP 63.4 bn $

L English, Kiswahili

↑ 58 / 68

Largest GDP in Southeast and Central Africa: national parks basis of tourism. Far more than 50 % of the population in the agriculture sector, but only 20 % of the land farmable; coffee, tea, sisal, roses (!), largest exporter of flowers worldwide since 2003.

Rwanda
Republic of Rwanda

★ Kigali
🏛 Unitary semi-presidential republic

👥 11,610,000
⬠ 26,400 km²
👪 440
GNI 700 $
GDP 8.1 bn $
L English, French, Kinyarwanda
↑ 74 / 52

Borders Burundi, catastrophic genocide by the Hutu on the Tutsi, coming to terms with it still underway. "Land of 1,000 hills," once marked by poverty and now economic success; in terms of politics, freedom of the press, free elections, and freedom of political opposition lacking.

REPUBLIKA Y'U RWANDA
REPUBLIC OF RWANDA
REPUPLIQUE DU RWANDA

URWANDIKO RW'ABAJYA MU MAHANGA
PASSPORT

Burundi
Republic of Burundi

★ Bujumbura
🏛 Presidential republic

👥 11,180,000
⬜ 27,800 km²
👪 402
GNI 260 $
GDP 3.1 bn $
ʟ French, Kirundi
↑ 80 / 46

Nearly 50 % of its citizens younger than 15, average age in the country: 16.7 yrs.! One of Africa's smallest countries, one of the most densely populated. Ethnic and language community of the Burundians: 85 % Hutu and 14 % Tutsi. Human rights situation problematical.

REPUBLIKA Y'UBURUNDI
REPUBLIQUE DU BURUNDI
REPUBLIC OF BURUNDI

IKITABU C'INZIRA
PASSEPORT DE SERVICE
SERVICE PASSPORT

Tanzania
United Republic of Tanzania

★ Dodoma
🏛 Unitary socialist presidential republic

👥 53,470,000
◻ 947,300 km²
👥 56
GNI 920 $
GDP 45.6 bn $
L English, Swahili
↑ 62 / 64

Country's name made up of TANganyika, ZAnzibar, and AzaNIA; 50 million inhabitants, 125 (!) languages, from Bantu and Arab to Indian languages; part of lakes Victoria, Tanganyika, and Malawi (three largest lakes); tallest mountain in Africa.

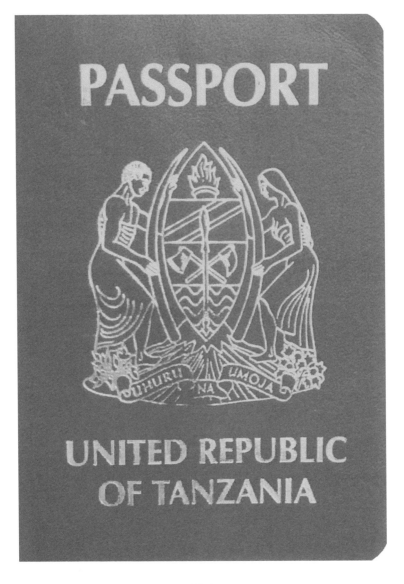

Angola
Republic of Angola

- ★ Luanda
- 🏛 Unitary presidential constitutional republic

- 👥 25,020,000
- ⬭ 1,246,700 km²
- 👥 20
- **GNI** 4,180 $
- **GDP** 102.6 bn $
- **L** Portuguese
- ↑ 80/46

Oil-rich dictatorship in a former Portuguese colony, whereby latent poverty prevails nationwide but the leadership clique hoards enormous wealth in the capital of Luanda, one of the most expensive cities in the world.

Zambia
Republic of Zambia

★ Lusaka
🏛 Unitary presidential republic

👥 16,210,000
🗺 752,600 km²
👪 22
GNI 1,490 $
GDP 21.2 bn $
L English
↑ 64 / 62

Plateaus with numerous river systems; Victoria Falls from
the "Zambezi" (eponym); the Congo river, many waterfalls,
20 national parks, among the countries with highest rate of
HIV worldwide.

Malawi
Republic of Malawi

★ Lilongwe
🏛 Unitary presidential republic

👥 17,220,000
⬜ 118,500 km²
⛪ 145
GNI 340 $
GDP 6.4 bn $
L Chichewa, English
↑ 59 / 67

Landlocked country on Lake Malawi, Africa's third-largest lake, ca. 14 million inhabitants comprised of diverse Bantu peoples, almost 12 % of all adults HIV-positive. Two million years ago already populated by the species "homo"; one of the poorest countries worldwide, widespread corruption.

Mozambique
Republic of Mozambique

★ Maputo
🏛 Unitary semi-presidential republic

👥 27,980,000
◻ 799,400 km²
👥 35
GNI 590 $
GDP 14.8 bn $
L Portuguese
↑ 74 / 52

Independent from Portugal since 1975; higher crime risk in cities. Tropical storms that can attain cyclone strength; cases of piracy off the cost; soil type mainly dry savanna; predominantly Bantu peoples; one of the highest rates of HIV in the world.

REPÚBLICA
DE
MOÇAMBIQUE

PASSAPORTE
PASSPORT

Namibia
Republic of Namibia

★ Windhoek
🏛 Unitary semi-presidential republic

👥 2,460,000
🗌 824,300 km²
🏛 3
GNI 5,190 $
GDP 11.5 bn $
ʟ English
↑ 60 / 66

One of the oldest parts of the earth's crust. Stable parliamentary democracy; agricultural sector, tourism, mining (uranium, gold, silver, and "non-precious" metals). Borders Botswana and the Kalahari; sand dunes in Namib Desert among the highest worldwide (up to 400 m).

REPUBLIC OF
NAMIBIA

UNITY LIBERTY JUSTICE

PASSPORT

Botswana
Republic of Botswana

★ Gaborone
🏛 Parliamentary republic

👥 2,260,000
⬜ 581,700 km²
👪 4
GNI 6,460 $
GDP 14.4 bn $
L English
↑ 55 / 72

Transparency International: Africa's lowest corruption rate.
Good development since independence from GB in 1966.
Model healthcare system in the surrounding area, but almost
20 % of all adults are HIV-positive. National parks are important tourist attraction.

REPUBLIC OF
BOTSWANA

OFFICIAL PASSPORT
PASSEPORT OFFICIEL

Zimbabwe
Republic of Zimbabwe

★ Harare

🏛 Unitary dominant-party
presidential republic

👥 15,600,000

▱ 390,700 km²

👪 40

GNI 860 $

GDP 14.4 bn $

L English and
16 regional languages

↑ 65 / 61

Mostly dry savanna, baobab and kigelia trees; de facto dictator Mugabe fights against domestic rivals; as regards foreign
policy, sanctions work against the regime, catastrophic economic situation. Always at the bottom of the happiness index.

South Africa
Republic of South Africa

★   Pretoria
🏛   Unitary parliamentary constitutional republic

👥   54,960,000
⬭   1,219,100 km²
👥   45
GNI   6,080 $
GDP   314.6 bn $
L   Afrikaans, English,
Northern Sotho,
Southern Sotho, Swazi, Tsonga,
Tswana, Venda, Xhosa, Zulu
↑   48 / 93

Africa's best-developed economy, one of the G-20 states; after 1945 decades of apartheid, overcome in 1994 with first free elections. "Rainbow nation" with any number of ancestries, hosted Africa's first soccer World Cup in 2010; magnificent nature.

REPUBLIC OF
SOUTH AFRICA

REPUBLIQUE
D'AFRIQUE DU SUD

PASSPORT

PASSEPORT

Lesotho
Kingdom of Lesotho

★ Maseru

🏛 Unitary parliamentary constitutional monarchy

👥 2,140,000

⬠ 30,300 km²

👥 71

GNI 1,280 $

GDP 2.3 bn $

L English, Sotho

↑ 57 / 69

The only country completely surrounded by another (South Africa), 6 out of 10 citizens are farmers; poverty, little vegetation, more than 30°C in the uplands (Drakensberg) in the summer (November to March), in the winter as low as -15°C; head of state is King Letsie III.

Swaziland
Kingdom of Swaziland

★ Mbabane
🏛 Unitary parliamentary absolute diarchy

👥 1,290,000
⬠ 17,400 km²
👪 74
GNI 3,280 $
GDP 4.1 bn $
L Swazi
↑ 59 / 67

Situated between Mozambique and South Africa, de facto
absolute monarchy. The king (*lion*) is head of the three state
authorities, his mother (*elephant mother*) his representative;
king also appoints head of government and himself lives in
luxury (eight Mercedes limousines).

Kingdom of Swaziland
Royaume de Swaziland
(ESWATINI)

SIYINQABA

PASSPORT
PASSEPORT

Cape Verde
Republic of Cabo Verde

★ Praia

🏛 Unitary semi-presidentialrepublic

👥 520,000

⬭ 4,040 km²

👥 129

GNI 3,280 $

GDP 1.6 bn $

L Portuguese

↑ 63 / 63

Nine inhabited volcanic islands almost 600 km off the Atlantic coast of Africa; uninhabited before being discovered, population comprises descendants of European settlers and African slaves; immigration from Portugal, emigration due to famine.

REPÚBLICA
DE
CABO VERDE

PASSAPORTE

São Tomé and Príncipe
Democratic Republic of
São Tomé and Príncipe

★ São Tomé
🏛 Unitary semi-presidential republic

👫 190,000
⬠ 1,000 km²
👪 190
GNI 1,760 $
GDP 3 bn $
L Portuguese
↑ 70 / 56

"St. Thomas and Prince"; after Seychelles Africa's second-smallest country; generates 40 % if its income from offshore drilling licenses (oil) administered with Nigeria. Affected by malaria. Marine fauna with several species of dolphins and whales; hot, humid climate.

REPÚBLICA DEMOCRÁTICA
DE SÃO TOMÉ E PRÍNCIPE

PASSAPORTE

Comoros
Union of the Comoros

★ Moroni
🏛 Federal presidential republic

👥 790,000
⬜ 1,860 km²
👥 425
GNI 780 $
GDP 565.7 bn $
L Comorian, French
↑ 76 / 50

Island state in the Indian Ocean between Madagascar and Mozambique; a good ³/₄ million inhabitants; "Mayotte," the fourth main island, is French but claimed by the "Union of the Comoros"; predominantly Muslim population of East African or Arab descent.

UNION DES COMORES

جمهورية القمر المتحدة

PASSEPORT

جواز سفر

Seychelles
Republic of Seychelles

★ Victoria

🏛 Unitary presidential republic

👥 90,000

◻ 450 km²

👪 200

GNI 14,760 $

GDP 1.4 bn $

ʟ English, French,
Seychellois Creole

↑ 26 / 128

Archipelago off the East African coast, north of Madagascar:
three species of giant tortoise, countless other endemic animal
species; parts are UNESCO World Heritage natural sites
(founded specifically for this reason); abundant birdlife, some
species of which only exist here.

Republic of Seychelles
République des Seychelles

PASSPORT
PASSEPORT

Madagascar
Republic of Madagascar

★ Antananarivo

🏛 Unitary semi-presidential constitutional republic

👥 24,240,000

⬜ 587,000 km²

👪 41

GNI 420 $

GDP 9.7 bn $

L French, Malagasy

↑ 75 / 51

In terms of surface area, second-largest island state world-wide after Indonesia. Regular hurricanes in first third of the year, abundant animal and plant world, but also infectious diseases, travellers recommended to be well immunised; country and its citizens very poor.

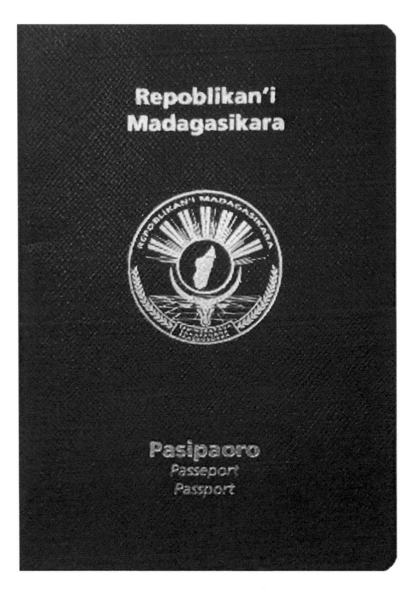

Repoblikan'i
Madagasikara

Pasipaoro
Passeport
Passport

Mauritius
Republic of Mauritius

★ Port Louis
🏛 Unitary parliamentary republic

👥 1,260,000
⬜ 2,040 km²
👪 618
GNI 9,780 $
GDP 11.7 bn $
L English
↑ 31 / 121

Islands in the Indian Ocean, popular among Europeans because of the "reversed" times of year. Only fruit bats lived there prior to colonization, humans introduced rats and mice, mongooses, monkeys, and ground game. More than 100 species of birds, ca. 15 tropical storms annually.

Republic of Mauritius

Passport

As

ia

Syria
Syrian Arab Republic

★ Damascus

🏛 Unitary dominant-party semi-presidentialrepublic

👥 18,500,000

⬭ 185,200 km²

👥 100

GNI 1,860 $ (2007)

GDP 40.4 bn $ (2007)

L Arabic

↑ 90/31

Just under 21 million inhabitants, of which (by March 2017) 5 million fled overseas from civil war, another 6 million internally displaced; Assad regime supported by Moscow and Iran fights against various rebel groups and the Islamic terror group IS.

الجمهورية العربية السورية

SYRIAN ARAB REPUBLIC

REPUBLIQUE ARABE SYRIENNE

جواز سفر

PASSPORT

PASSEPORT

Lebanon
Lebanese Republic

★ Beirut
🏛 Unitary parliamentary
multi-convessionalist republic

👥 5,850,000
⬜ 10,500 km²
👥 557
GNI 7,710 $
GDP 47.1 bn $
L Arabic
↑ 87 / 38

"Cedar State" (tree in national flag and widespread in the country); capital Beirut (every second Lebanese lives here) once "Paris of the Middle East," destruction in decade of civil war between representatives of Syria/Iran/the Palestine Territories vs. Israel.

Israel
State of Israel

★ Jerusalem
🏛 Unitary parliamentary constitutional republic

👥 8,380,000
◻ 20,800 km²
🏙 403
GNI 35,770 $
GDP 299.4 bn $
ʟ Arabic, Hebrew
↑ 19 / 138

Only Western-style democracy in the Middle East, with the US as a protecting power. Palestinians perceived the influx of Jewish refugees (in particular from Nazi Germany) as a provocation; the "Middle East Conflict" has prevailed since.

Palestinian Territories

★ Ramallah
🏛 De jure parliamentary republic
operatin de facto as a semi-presidential
republic

👥 4,420,000
◻ 6,020 km²
👥 734
GNI 3,090 $ (2014)
GDP 12.7 bn $
L Arabic
↑ 86 / 39

One of the most densely populated regions on earth; half the
population extremely poor. Israel responds to terror attacks
with bombs on the homes of suspected assassins. State territory divided into the West Bank, East Jerusalem, and the
Gaza Strip.

Jordan
The Hashemite Kingdom of Jordan

★ Amman
🏛 Unitary parliamentary constitutional monarchy

👥 7,590,000
⬭ 89,300 km²
👪 85
GNI 4,680 $
GDP 37.5 bn $
L Arabic
↑ 79 / 47

Hereditary monarchy; father of the current king already found path to peaceful neighbourship with Israel. Ca. 10 million inhabitants, of which ca. 2 million are Palestinians; influx of refugees (due to war with Israel, both Gulf Wars against Iraq and, civil war in Syria).

المملكة الأردنية الهاشمية

THE HASHEMITE KINGDOM OF JORDAN

جواز سفر

PASSPORT

Saudi Arabia
Kingdom of Saudi Arabia

★ Riyadh
🏛 Unitary Islamic abolute monarchy
    under totalitarian dictatorship

👥 31,540,000
◰ 2,149,700 km²
👪 15
GNI 23,550 $
GDP 646 bn $
L Arabic
↑ 57 / 69

Strategically important for the West, absolutist royal house calls itself the guardian of the holy sites of Mecca and Medina; ancient interpretation of sharia, human rights violations the order of the day, oil power, working world sustained by foreign workers.

الملكة العربية السعودية

KINGDOM OF SAUDI ARABIA

عضو جامعة الدول العربية

جواز سفر

PASSPORT

Yemen
Republic of Yemen

★ Sana'a

🏛 Provisional government

👥 26,830,000

◠ 528,100 km²

👥 51

GNI 1,140 bn $

GDP 37.7 $

L Arabic

↑ 88 / 37

In the south of the Arab Peninsula, access to the Red and the Arabian Sea; Shiite Hutu rebels, supporters of the ex-president, and remaining Al Qaida groups fight against the government; Saudi Arabia and eight additional countries intervened, since then war.

REPUBLIC OF YEMEN

PASSPORT

327

Oman
Sultanate of Oman

★ Mascat
🏛 Unitary parliamentary
absolute monarchy

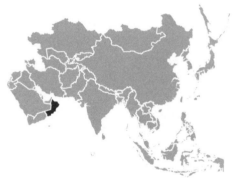

👫 4,490,000
◻ 309,500 km²
👫 15
GNI 16,910 $
GDP 69.8 bn $
L Arabic
↑ 56/71

Oil-rich absolute monarchy; practices "Omanisation," the replacement of foreign workers with locals; ³/₄ of the population are Ibadi Muslims, who constitute the majority only here, neither Sunni nor Shia but an independent Islamic school of religious jurisprudence.

United Arabic Emirates

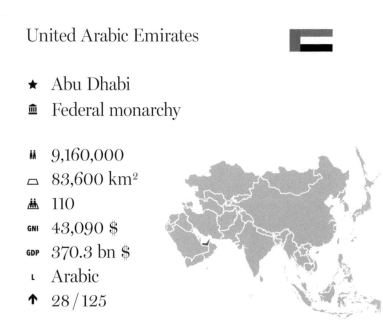

★ Abu Dhabi
🏛 Federal monarchy

👬 9,160,000
◻ 83,600 km²
👪 110
GNI 43,090 $
GDP 370.3 bn $
L Arabic
↑ 28 / 125

Dubai and Abu Dhabi (*father of the gazelle*) known interna-
tionally; furthermore includes the emirates of Sharjah, Ajman,
Umm al-Quwain (*mother of two powers*), Ras al-Khaimah (*top
of tent*), and Fujairah; oil, gas, financial services, building and
real estate sector.

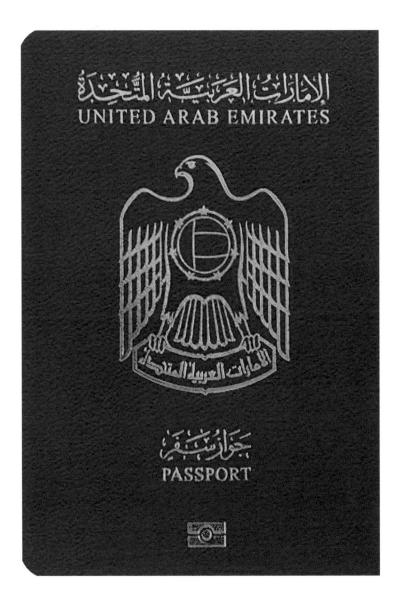

Qatar
State of Qatar

★ Doha
🏛 Unitary constitutional monarchy

👥 2,240,000
⬜ 11,400 km²
👪 196
GNI 83,990 $
GDP 164.6 bn $
L Arabic
↑ 51/78

Hereditary monarchy (legal basis sharia); one of the driest countries in the world; "salt flats," drinking water has to be desalinised; only every seventh citizen a native; violation of human rights (women/foreign workers), sells oil, natural gas, rest areas for the US Army.

STATE OF QATAR

PASSPORT

Bahrain
Kingdom of Bahrain

★ Manama
🏛 Unitary parliamentary constitutional monarchy

👥 1,380,000
◻ 720 km²
👥 1,917
GNI 19,840 $
GDP 31.1 bn $
L Arabic
↑ 53/75

Thirty-three islands in the Persian Gulf, territory (extended by earth fills) about as big as Hamburg (without surrounding areas). Desert climate; few animal species; natives and immigrants (mostly foreign workers) approximately equal parts of the total population.

مملكة البحرين

KINGDOM OF BAHRAIN

جواز سفر

PASSPORT

Kuwait
State of Kuwait

★ Kuwait City
🏛 Unitary constitutional monarchy

👥 3,890,000
⬠ 17,800 km²
👥 219
GNI 42,150 $
GDP 114 bn $
L Arabic
↑ 50 / 84

The Arabian Desert covers most of the country; land of oil, USA protecting power, after the Iraqi invasion of 1990/91 exempt from the Western "Coalition of the Gulf War." Only about 30 % of the inhabitants are free total-care Kuwaitis, the rest are foreign workers.

Iraq
Republic of Iraq

★ Baghdad
🏛 Federal parliamentary republic

👥 36,420,000
⬜ 438,300 km²
👪 83
GNI 5,820 $
GDP 180.1 bn $
L Arabic,
  Kurdish
↑ 91 / 28

After the war against Iran between 1980 and 1988 (the USA supported Saddam Hussein) overrun twice by the USA with war: after the occupation of Kuwait in 1990–91 and then in 2003. The result: permanent instability, Islamist terror. World oil power.

Iran
Islamic Republic of Iran

★ Teheran

🏛 Islamic republic

👫 79,110,000

◻ 1,648,000 km²

👪 48

GNI 6550 $ (2014)

GDP 423.3 bn $ (2014)

L Persian (Farsi)

↑ 88 / 37

Shia theocracy, governed by the "Guardian Council of the Revolution," which expelled the Shah in the late 1970s and turned away from the USA and toward the USSR. World oil power. Non-Arab nation, Shia second-largest Islamic movement.

Afghanistan
Islamic Republic of Afghanistan

★ Kabul

🏛 Unitary presidential Islamic republic

👥 32,530,000

⬚ 652,200 km²

👥 50

GNI 610 $

GDP 19.3 bn $

L Dari, Pashto

↑ 93 / 24

Barren high plateau, where the USSR experienced its "Vietnam" in the early 1980s. Islamist regimes subsequently spread; however, they were repeatedly attacked by warlord-led troops from different regions of the country.

دافغانستان اسلامي جمهوريت پاسپورت

جمهوری اسلامی افغانستان پاسپورت

ISLAMIC REPUBLIC
OF AFGHANISTAN
PASSPORT

343

Pakistan
Islamic Republic of Pakistan

★ Islamabad

🏛 Federal parliamentary constitutional republic

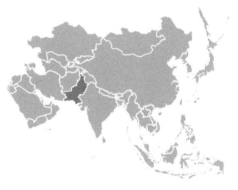

👥 188,920,000

▱ 796,100 km²

👥 237

GNI 1,440 $

GDP 271.1 bn $

L English, Urdu

↑ 92 / 27

Politically extremely unstable nuclear power, cultivates permanent hostility toward neighboring India, above all concerning the region of Kashmir. Retreat area for the Taliban, Al Qaida, and IS fighters; repeated coups by the army.

India
Republic of India

★ New Delhi
🏛 Federal parliamenary constitutional
republic

👥 1,311.050,000
⬭ 3,287,300 km²
👪 399
GNI 1,600 $
GDP 2,095.4 bn $
L English,
Hindi and 22 regional languages
↑ 78 / 48

After China the second nation with a population of over a billion, calls itself the "largest democracy in the world"; more than 100 languages, largest religious groups: Hindus, Muslims, Christians, Sikhs. Society with "caste" system. Chaotic megacities.

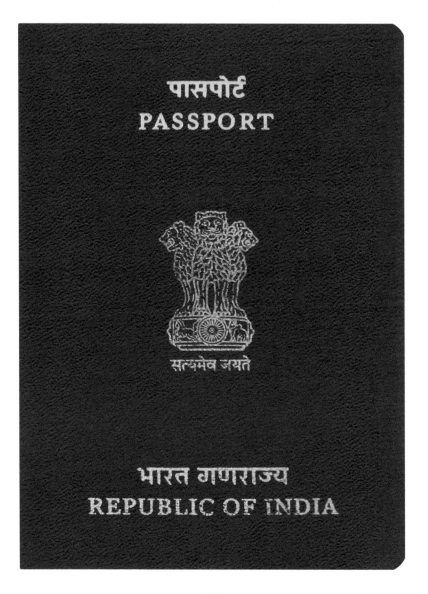

Nepal
Federal Democratic Republic of Nepal

★ Kathmandu

🏛 Federal parliamentary republic

👥 28.510,000

⬜ 147,200 km²

👪 194

GNI 730 $

GDP 21.2 bn $

L Nepali

↑ 88 / 37

Caste society with an illiteracy rate of 50 %; the "highest" caste (Brahmans) does not acknowledge 70 % of the remaining population. Situated between China and India, Nepal has a share of 8 of the 10 highest mountains in the world (Himalayas), alpine tourism.

राहदानी
नेपाल

PASSPORT
NEPAL

Bhutan
Kingdom of Bhutan

★ Thimphu

🏛 Unitary parliamentaryconstitutional monarchy

👥 770,000

⬜ 38,400 km²

👥 20

GNI 2,380 $

GDP 2.1 bn $

ʟ Dzongkha

↑ 76 / 50

Situated between India and China (Tibet), about as large as Switzerland, only higher mountains (Himalayas). Forest covers ²/₃ of the country, abundant animal world, tiger sightings at more than 4,000 m above sea level. Two mountains that have never been scaled by humans.

KINGDOM OF BHUTAN

PASSPORT

Bangladesh
People's Republic of Bangladesh

★ Dhaka

🏛 Unitary parliamentaryrepublic

👥 161,000,000

⬭ 147,600 km²

👥 1,091

GNI 1,190 $

GDP 195.1

L Bangladeshi

↑ 88 / 37

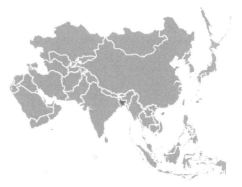

"East Bengal," which broke away in the course of Indian independence specifically for Muslims; extensive slums here as well, flood disasters and famine, long reliant on aid from the UN, today far better developed economically, primarily the result of textile production with problematic substandard wages.

Maldives
Republic of Maldives

★ Male

🏛 Unitary parliamentary constitutional republic

👥 410.000

⬠ 300 km²

👥 1,367

GNI 6,950 $

GDP 3.4 bn $

L Maldivian (Divehi)

↑ 54/74

Name means "island chain," state territory 1,196 islands, of which 220 are inhabited, tourism on just fewer than 90 other islands. Mild, stable tropical climate year round, rarely monsoons; Sunni Islam predominant; literacy rate 99%.

Sri Lanka
Democratic Socialist Republic of Sri Lanka

★ Colombo
🏛 Unitary semi-presidential constitutional republic

👥 20,970,000
⬜ 65,600 km²
👪 320
GNI 3,800 $
GDP 82.3 bn $
L Sinhalese, Tamil
↑ 87/38

Tea, coffee, rubber, and coconut dominate exports; national languages: Sinhala and Tamil. Home of the Ayurveda art of healing, meantime popular vacation island, previously politically unstable due to civil war between Tamil rebels and the central government.

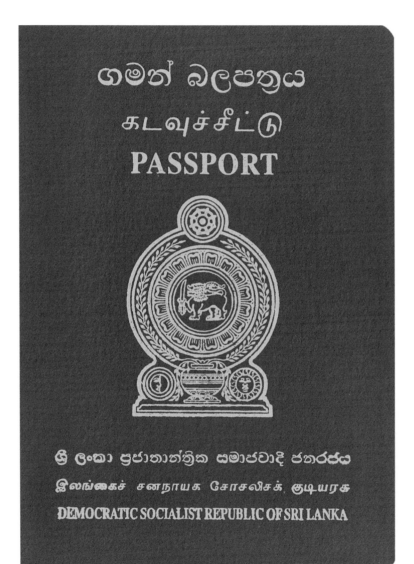

ගමන් බලපත්‍රය

கடவுச்சீட்டு

PASSPORT

ශ්‍රී ලංකා ප්‍රජාතාන්ත්‍රික සමාජවාදි ජනරජය

இலங்கைச் சனநாயக சோசலிசக் குடியரசு

DEMOCRATIC SOCIALIST REPUBLIC OF SRI LANKA

Kazakhstan
Republic of Kazakhstan

★ Astana

🏛 Unitary dominant-party presidential republic

👥 17,540,000

⬠ 2,724,900 km²

👪 6

GNI 11,390 $

GDP 184.4 bn $

L Kazakh, Russian

↑ 57/69

Former Soviet republic whose expanses provided room for the USSR's spaceflight program; funnily enough, building and shooting down model rockets is still a popular sport and is presented in large stadiums at every level of competition, all the way to world championships.

ҚАЗАҚСТАН
РЕСПУБЛИКАСЫ
REPUBLIC OF
KAZAKHSTAN

ПАСПОРТ
PASSPORT

Turkmenistan

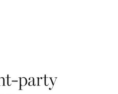

★ Asgabat

🏛 Unitary dominant-party
presidential republic

👥 5,370,000

◻ 488,100 km²

🏛 11

GNI 7,380 $

GDP 35.9 bn $

L Turkmen

↑ 77/47

Central Asian state at the Caspian Sea; 95 % of the land
surface is sand and gravel deserts; extremely hot, dry summers and ice-cold winters. Primarily Muslim; head of state
also president of both chambers of parliament; former Soviet
republic.

Uzbekistan
Republic of Uzbekistan

★ Tashkent

🏛 Unitary presidential constitutional republic

👬 31,300,000

⬭ 447,400 km²

👪 70

GNI 2,160 $

GDP 66.7 bn $

L Usbek

↑ 72 / 54

Central Asian landlocked nation with moderate climate despite large desert and steppe areas, abundant fauna and flora; secular state. Water removal from the Amu Darya and Syr Darya rivers lead to the drying up of the Aral Sea and to extreme soil salinisation.

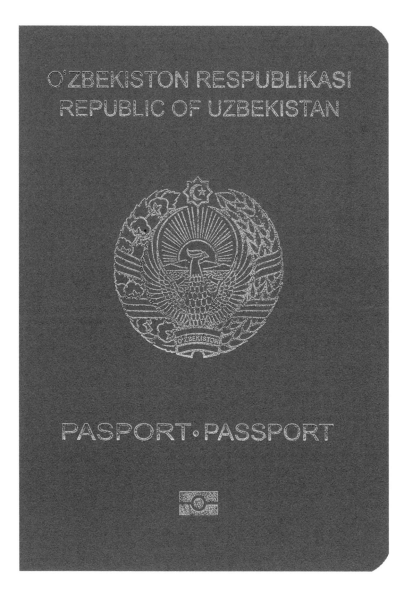

O'ZBEKISTON RESPUBLIKASI
REPUBLIC OF UZBEKISTAN

PASPORT · PASSPORT

Kyrgyzstan
Kyrgyz Republic

★ Bishkek
🏛 Unitary parliamentary republic

👥 5,960,000
◰ 199,900 km²
👪 30
GNI 1,170 $
GDP 6.6
L Kyrgyz, Russian
↑ 68 / 58

Former Soviet republic, since its collapse independent, largest walnut forests in the world, after the "Tulip Revolution" in 2005 strengthening of democratic forces, constitution gives the president a great deal of power, the judiciary often under political pressure.

КЫРГЫЗ РЕСПУБЛИКАСЫ

КЫРГЫЗСКАЯ РЕСПУБЛИКА

THE KYRGYZ REPUBLIC

ПАСПОРТ

ПАСПОРТ

PASSPORT

Tajikistan
Republic of Tajikistan

★ Dushanbe
🏛 Unitary dominant-party
    presidential republic

👥 8,480,000
⬜ 143,100 km²
👥 59
GNI 1,280 $
GDP 7.9 bn $
L Tajik
↑ 72 / 54

Main religion Sunni Islam; the rest a blend ranging from
"Seventh-day Adventists" to "Ismailis." German minority has
markedly declined since the collapse of the Soviet Union;
every fourth girl does not complete compulsory primary
school due to gender-specific discrimination.

ҶУМҲУРИИ
ТОҶИКИСТОН

REPUBLIC OF TAJIKISTAN

ШИНОСНОМА

PASSPORT

Mongolia

★ Ulan-Bator
🏛 Unitary semi-presidential republic

👥 2,960,000
⬠ 1,564,100 km²
👥 2
GNI 3,870 $
GDP 11.7 bn $
L Mongolian
↑ 68 / 58

One of the most sparsely populated countries on earth, statistically speaking, 1 km² for every two Mongolians; nomadic people; huge reindeer herds, antlers go to China as a potency remedy; large-scale alcohol problem and enormous Genghis Khan monuments.

China
People's Republic of China

★ Beijing
🏛 Unitary one-party socialist republic

👥 1,371,220,000
⬜ 9,572,400 km²
👪 143
GNI 7,930 $
GDP 11,007.7 bn $
L Standard Chinese
↑ 70 / 56

Every sixth human being on earth lives here, governed by probably the only Wild-West-capitalistic communist party in the world; the turbo-economy in the "special economic zones" is accompanied by the continuation of widespread poverty in rural areas.

North Korea
Democratic People's Republic of Korea

★ Pyongyang
🏛 Hereditary Juche one-party state under a totalitarian dictatorship

👪 25,150,000
◰ 122,800 km²
👥 205
GNI n.d.
GDP n.d.
L Korean
↑ 86 / 39

Since 1948 developed by the USSR into a centralized communist state. Influx of Koreans from eastern Soviet republics; today terror dictatorship; personality cult around leader, economy of scarcity, hunger, and oppression; army provokes by launching test rockets.

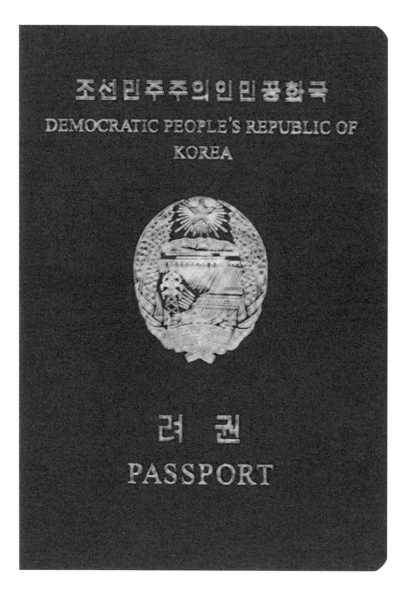

South Korea
Republic of Korea

★ Seoul

🏛 Unitary presidential constitutional republic

👥 50,620,000

⌂ 99,300 km²

⛪ 510

GNI 27,450 $

GDP 1,377.9 bn $

L Korean

↑ 4 / 157

East Asian "tiger state" par excellence after World War II. Rapid economic development, under US protection development into a capitalistic democracy after war against North Korea/USSR. Densely populated, automobile and IT production, TV, HiFi, microchips.

Japan

★ Tokyo
🏛 Unitary parliamentary constitutional monarchy

👥 126,960,000
⌂ 378,000 km²
👪 336
GNI 38,840 $
GDP 4,383.1 bn $
L Japanese
↑ 5 / 156

Very old imperial dynasty; Western democracy since World War II, when Japan was Nazi Germany's ally. Leading high-tech country for a long time, today a tottering economy; Fukushima reactor accident in 2001 lead to Germany's nuclear power phase-out.

日本国旅券

JAPAN

PASSPORT

Macau

★ Macau

🏛 Special administrative region

👥 580,000

⬯ 24 km²

👪 24,167

GNI 67,180 $

GDP 46.2 bn $

L Cantonese, Portuguese

↑ 33/118

Macau belonged to Portugal until 1999. Portuguese has remained the official language. Nearly 600,000 people are squeezed together here on just less than 24 km².

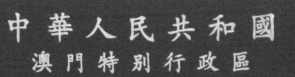

中華人民共和國
澳門特別行政區

REGIÃO ADMINISTRATIVA ESPECIAL DE MACAU
REPÚBLICA POPULAR DA CHINA

MACAO SPECIAL ADMINISTRATIVE REGION
PEOPLE'S REPUBLIC OF CHINA

護　照

PASSAPORTE
PASSPORT

Hong Kong

★ Hong Kong
🏛 Special administrative region

👥 7,310,000
⬜ 1,100 km²
👪 6,645
GNI 41,000 $
GDP 309.2
ʟ Traditional Chinese,
English
↑ 18 / 140

China grants Hong Kong, which like Macau belonged to Portugal until 1999, a high degree of autonomy, apart from in the areas of foreign and defense policy.

Taiwan
Republic of China

★ Taipeh
🏛 Unitary semi-presidential
constitutional republic

👥 23,430,000
◻ 36,000 km²
👪 651
GNI n.d.
GDP n.d.
ʟ Traditional Chinese
(Putonghua)
↑ 32 / 120

The small island ("Republic of China") off the coast of the huge Red China was a sanctuary for Chiang Kai-shek after conflict with troops led by Mao Tse-tung. Before that, the inhabitants of the former "Formosa" were not Chinese; Beijing sees Taiwan as its property.

Myanmar
Republic of the Union of Myanmar

★ Naypyidaw
🏛 Unitary parliamentary constitutional republic

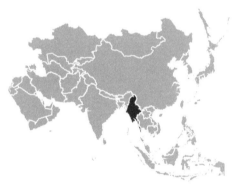

👥 53,900,000
⬭ 676,600 km²
👥 80
GNI 1,160 $
GDP 62.6 bn $
L Burmese
↑ 85 / 41

Formerly "Burma," fighting between rebel groups and the military government, which appointed the civilian head of state; yet democratization faltering, ethnic tensions, predominately Buddhist, frequent natural disasters due to monsoons and earthquakes.

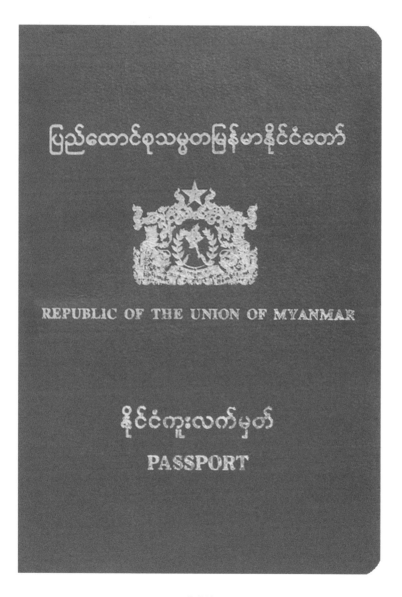

REPUBLIC OF THE UNION OF MYANMAR

PASSPORT

Laos
Lao People's Democratic Republic

★ Vientiane

🏛 Unitary Marxist-Leninist
one-party communist republic

👥 6,800,000

⌐ 236,800 km²

👥 29

GNI 1,740 $

GDP 12.4 bn $

L Lao

↑ 79 / 47

(Rice) farmers make up 80 % of the population; numerous
rivers serve as traffic routes. The once enormous wild elephant
population has dropped to about 500. Human rights violations despite guaranteed basic rights such as, for example, the
freedom of religion.

ສາທາລະນະລັດ ປະຊາທິປະໄຕ ປະຊາຊົນລາວ
République Démocratique Populaire Lao
Lao People's Democratic Republic

ໜັງສືຜ່ານແດນ
PASSPORT
PASSPORT

Vietnam
Socialist Republic of Vietnam

★ Hanoi

🏛 Marxist-Leninist one-party
   socialist republic

👥 91,700,000

⌂ 331,200 km²

👪 277

GNI 1,990 $

GDP 193.6

L Vietnamese

↑ 77/47

In the 20th century scene of the exemplary proxy war that
divided the country in to the pro-US south and the north,
which was supported by the USSR and China.

CỘNG HÒA XÃ HỘI CHỦ NGHĨA VIỆT NAM
SOCIALIST REPUBLIC OF VIETNAM

HỘ CHIẾU
PASSPORT

389

Thailand
Kingdom of Thailand

★ Bangkok

🏛 Unitary parliamentary constitutional monarchy

👥 67,960,000

⬭ 513,100 km²

🏛 132

GNI 5,720 $

GDP 395.2 bn $

L Thai

↑ 55 / 72

Set up its tourism sector during the Vietnam War when US soldiers came here on R&R; the beloved King Bhumibol died in 2016, his successor, his son, is controversial, party landscape rutted and unstable, separatist rebels in the Muslim south.

Cambodia
Kingdom of Cambodia

★ Phnom Penh

🏛 Unitary dominant-party parliamentaryelective constitutional monarchy

👪 15,580,000

⬜ 181,000 km²

👪 86

GNI 1,070 $

GDP 18.1 bn $

L Khmer

↑ 77 / 47

Pulled into the Vietnam War after carpet bombing by the US, the country fell into the hands of the stone-age communist regime of the "Red Khmer"—systematic mass murder of an entire generation meant to create a new world—coping with trauma continues.

ព្រះរាជាណាចក្រកម្ពុជា

KINGDOM OF CAMBODIA
ROYAUME DU CAMBODGE

លិខិតឆ្លងដែន

PASSPORT
PASSEPORT

Philippines
Republic of the Philippines

★ Manila

🏛 Unitary presidential constitutional republic

👥 100,700,000

⬜ 300,000 km²

👥 336

GNI 3,550 $

GDP 292.5 bn $

L Filipino

↑ 65 / 61

Over 7,000 individual islands, separatist rebel groups that carry out attacks and abductions. Influenced by Catholicism since its discovery by Spanish colonists in 1543, named in honour of the then Spanish Crown Prince Philip, later King Philip II.

Malaysia

- ★ Kuala Lumpur
- 🏛 Federal parliamentary elective constitutional monarchy

- ⚥ 30,330,000
- ◻ 329,800 km²
- ⚥ 92
- GNI 10,570 $
- GDP 296.3 bn $
- ʟ Malay (Bahasa Malaysia)
- ↑ 6/155

Economically a "threshold state," export: tin, palm oil, rubber, oil. Two domestic car manufacturers; two regions, separated by the South China Sea: the Malaysian Peninsula in the west (majority of the population) and the island of Borneo.

Singapore
Republic of Singapore

★ Singapore
🏛 Unitary dominant-party
parliamentary republic

👥 5.540,000
⬓ 720 km²
👥 7,694
GNI 52,090 $
GDP 292.7 bn $
L English, Malay,
Mandarin, Tamil
↑ 3 / 158

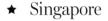

City-state at the southern tip of the Malaysian Peninsula;
strong republican-democratic system; draconian punishment
for petty offenses. One of the countries with the highest cost
of living worldwide.

Brunei
Nation of Brunei

★ Bandar Seri Begawan

🏛 Unitary Islamic absolute monarchy

👥 420,000

⬜ 5,770 km²

👥 73

GNI 38,010 $

GDP 12.9 bn$

L Malay

↑ 20 / 136

Sultanate on the island of Borneo in the South China Sea; independent from the UK since 1984. The sultan resides in the largest palace in the world, estimated fortune: US $20 billion; knighted by the Queen, 12 children with 3 wives.

Indonesia
Republic of Indonesia

★ Jakarta
🏛 Unitary presidential
constitutional republic

👫 257.560,000
◠ 1,913,000 km²
👪 135
GNI 3,440 $
GDP 861.9 bn $
L Indonesian
↑ 67 / 59

With over 255 million people, the most populous Muslim country in the world; world's largest island state with more than 17,000 islands. More than half the population lives on the main island of Java, one of the first Dutch colonies.

REPUBLIK INDONESIA

PASPOR

PASSPORT

East Timor
Democratic Republic
of Timor-Leste

★ Dili

🏛 Unitary semi-presidential republic

👥 1,250,000

▱ 14,900 km²

👪 84

GNI 2,180 $

GDP 1.4 bn $

L Portuguese, Tetum

↑ 50 / 84

Only Asian country with all of its terrain south of the equator, first country to achieve independence (from Indonesia) in the 21st century. Eastern part of the Indonesian island of Timor; long civil war; stabile today; former Portuguese colony.

REPÚBLICA DEMOCRÁTICA DE TIMOR-LESTE

PASSAPORTE

Aust
Oce

Australia
Commonwealth of Australia

★ Canberra
🏛 Federal parliamentary constitutional monarchy

👥 23,780,000
⬭ 7,692,000 km²
👥 3
GNI 60,070 $
GDP 1,339.1 bn $
L English
↑ 7 / 154

An entire continent for 20-some million people, nearly all of whom recently immigrated there. Only the indigenous people, the Aborigines, can refer back to a really long tradition.

Palau
Republic of Palau

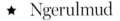

★ Ngerulmud

🏛 Unitary presidential constitutional republic and non-partisan democracy

👥 20,000

⬜ 500 km²

👥 40

GNI 12,180 $

GDP 0.3 bn $

L English, Palauan

↑ 46 / 101

Nation comprised of 356 islands in the Pacific; the ca. 22,000 inhabitants are distributed over 11 of the islands. Independent since 1994 but still associated with the colonial power of the USA; during World War II the site of fierce fighting between Japan and the USA.

Micronesia
Federated States of Micronesia

★ Palikir
🏛 Federal parliamentary republic under a nonpartisan democracy

👥 100,000
⬜ 700 km²
👪 143
GNI 3,560 $
GDP 0.3 bn $
L English
↑ 46 / 101

Statistically speaking, the fattest people worldwide live here and on Nauru due to customary diet. Politically predominant ethnic group: Chuukese. Seven official languages: English, Pohnpaeic, Kosraean, Yapese, Chuukic, Ulithian, Wolealan.

PASSPORT

Federated States of
Micronesia

413

Nauru
Republic of Nauru

★ Yaren

🏛 Non-partisan democracy, parliamentary republic

👥 10,000

⬠ 21 km²

👥 476

GNI 15,420 $

GDP 0.1 bn $

L English, Nauruan

↑ 56 / 71

Smallest republic on earth; lived well and for a long time from guano (phosphate mining), at the time it had the highest income per capita worldwide. Natural resource depleted: financial crisis, now legally competent as the result of foreign aid.

REPUBLIC
OF
NAURU

PASSPORT

Marshall Islands
Republic of the Marshall Islands

★ Majuro

🏛 Unitary parliamentary republic

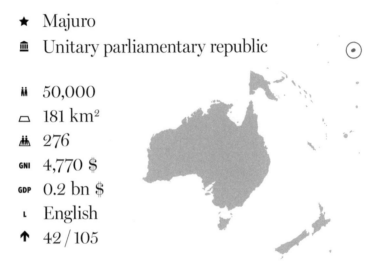

👥 50,000

◻ 181 km²

👪 276

GNI 4,770 $

GDP 0.2 bn $

L English

↑ 42 / 105

Independent since 1986, before that UN territory administered by the US; islands in part only two meters above sea
level; part of "Micronesia." Bikini Atoll was used for nuclear
bomb testing; rainy season May to November, otherwise hot,
humid climate; "tax haven."

Kiribati
Republic of Kiribati

★ Bairiki
🏛 Parliamentary republic

👥 110,000
⬜ 810 km²
👪 136
GNI 3,390 $
GDP 1.6 bn $
L English,
  Gilbertese
↑ 41 / 107

Archipelago in the Pacific with an overall expanse of 5.2 million km², thus one of the largest island nations in the world; ca. 110,000 inhabitants, highest athletic achievement: gold medal for weight lifter David Katoatau at the Commonwealth Games 2014.

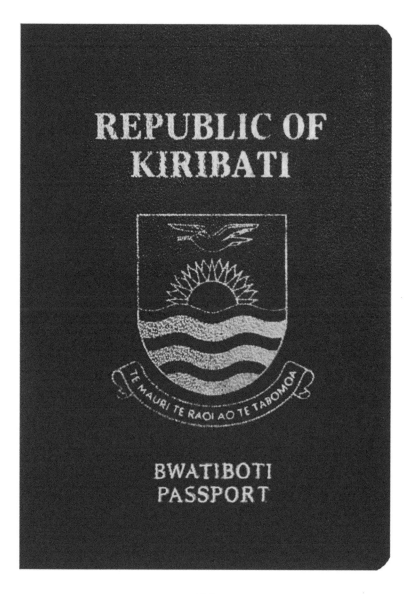

REPUBLIC OF
KIRIBATI

TE MAURI TE RAOI AO TE TABOMOA

BWATIBOTI
PASSPORT

Papua New Guinea
Independent State of
Papua New Guinea

★ Port Moresby
🏛 Unitary parliamentary constitutional monarchy

👥 7,620,000
▭ 462,800 km²
👪 16
GNI 2,240 $ (2014)
GDP 16.9 bn $ (2014)
L English, Hiri Motu, Tok Pisin
↑ 57 / 69

In terms of surface area, third-largest island nation in the world after Indonesia and Madagascar; complementary currency is the shell money "tolai." Only shell bank worldwide since 2002. Hard currency: "kina"; highly critical human rights situation.

420

PASSPORT

Papua New Guinea

Solomon Islands

★ Honiara

🏛 Unitary parliamentary constitutional monarchy

👥 580,000

◠ 27,600 km²

👪 21

GNI 1,920 $

GDP 1.1 bn $

L English

↑ 36 / 113

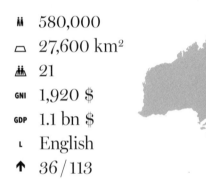

Island state in the South Sea (cultural sphere of Melanesia); member of the Commonwealth. Ethnic conflicts between Melanesians, Polynesians, and Micronesians from 1998 to 2003, decline in tourism, today visitors primarily from Australia and New Zealand.

SOLOMON ISLANDS

TO LEAD IS TO SERVE

PASSPORT

Tuvalu

★ Funafuti

🏛 Non-partisan parliamentary democracy und constitutional monarchy

👫 10,000

◻ 30 km²

👪 333

GNI 6,230 $

GDP 0.03 bn $

ʟ English, Tuvaluan

↑ 38 / 111

Polynesian island state in the South Pacific; independent since 1978. Official languages: Tuvaluan, English, Samoan, and Kiribati or Gilbertese; has no army of its own, sold rights to top-level domain "TV" and received IT technology and UN admission fee.

PASSPORT

TUVALU

Samoa
Independent State Samoa

★ Apia
🏛 Unitary parliamentary republic

👥 190,000
◰ 2,830 km²
👥 67
GNI 3,930 $
GDP 0.8 bn $
L English,
Samoan
↑ 37/112

Polynesian island state; independent from New Zealand since 1962. Traditional whole-body tattoos; plantation economy; industry: auto parts, building material from domestic timbers, cigarette production using imported tobacco. Popular sport "rugby union."

Vanuatu
Republic of Vanuatu

★ Port Vila
🏛 Unitary parliamentary republic

👥 270,000
⬜ 12,200 km²
👥 22
GNI 3,170 $ (2014)
GDP 0.7 bn $
L Bislama, English,
  French
↑ 35 / 115

Independent republic (since 1980) in the South Pacific, volcanic atoll. France and GB shared the administration of what at the time were the "New Hebrides"; currently problematical: overfishing, deforestation, shortage of drinking water (due to locals). Several active volcanoes.

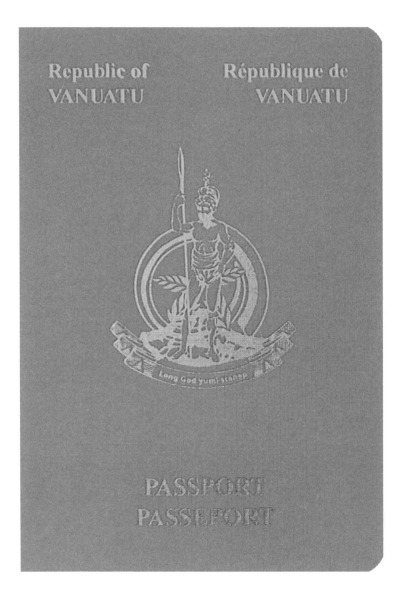

Fiji
Republic of Fiji

★ Suva

🏛 Unitary parlamentary
constitutional republic

👥 890,000

◻ 18,300 km²

👪 49

GNI 4,830 $

GDP 4.4 bn $

L English,
Fijian, Hindi

↑ 51/78

Parliamentary democracy since 2014; isolated archipelago
in the South Pacific, more than 2,000 km to New Zealand.
Mangroves on the coast, topical rainforest or savannas;
distinct animal and plant world; heads chair of the 23rd
UN Climate Conference in Bonn in 2017.

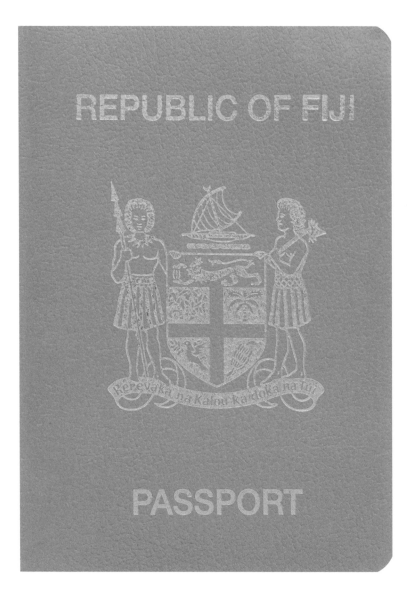

REPUBLIC OF FIJI

PASSPORT

Tonga
Kingdom of Tonga

★ Nuku'alofa
🏛 Unitary parliamentary
   constitutional monarchy

👫 110,000
⬜ 750 km²
⛰ 147
GNI 4,280 $
GDP 0.4 bn $
L Tongan
↑ 40 / 109

Polynesian archipelago in the South Pacific; ideal of beauty leads to endemic obesity, government therefore issues programs for diet counselling. Popular sport "rugby union"; best players after Australia and New Zealand.

PULE'ANGA 'O TONGA
KINGDOM OF TONGA

PAASIPOOTI
PASSPORT

New Zealand

★ Wellington
🏛 Unitary parliamentary
constitutional monarchy

👥 4,560,000
◻ 270,500 km²
👪 17
GNI 40,020 $
GDP 173.8 bn $
L English, Maori
↑ 7/154

Island nation far in the south of the Pacific (northern and southern island, then numerous smaller ones) "Oceania," great deal of natural diversity, sparsely populated, indigenous people (Maori). Strong agricultural sector: sheep farming, wine, fruit, fishing, main trade with Australia and China.

PORT 235F

DEPARTED AUSTRALIA
3 NOV 2004

IMMIGRATION
BANGKOK THAILAND
VISACLASS
2 5 FEB 2005
ADMITTED
UNTIL 2 6 MAR 2005
SIGNED
1379A1379A1379A1379A1379A

IMMIGRATION BANGKOK AUSTRALIA
DEPARTED
28 FEB 2005
SIGNED
A1180A1180A1180A1180A

POLICIA DE INVESTIGACIONES
CONTROL MIGRATORIO
1 0 SEP 04
CHILE
HUMBERTO A. MERINO BENITT

CAMBODIA IMMIGRATION
DEPARTED
2 9 JAN 2005
CODE 034013

2 5 1 3 2
PRAZO
DOC.
10 09 04 5 1 3
CLAS.

PMAF - DPF - BRASIL
PRAZO
DOC.
04 09 04 5 1 3

Passportindex

Place

47	Albania
48	South Africa
49	Ukraine
50	Belize, Kuwait and East Timor
51	Fiji, Jamaica, Qatar
52	Ecuador and Guyana
53	Bahrain
54	Maldives
55	Botswana and Thailand
56	Nauru and Oman
57	Kazakhstan, Lesotho, Papua new Guinea, Saudi Arabia and Suriname
58	Bolivia, Kenya and Belarus
59	Malawi and Swaziland
60	Namibia
61	Gambia
62	Tanzania
63	Azerbaijan and Cap Verde
64	Zambia and Tunesia
65	Philippines and Zimbabwe
66	Dominican Republic, Cuba, Sierra Leone and Uganda
67	Armenia, Ghana and Indonesia
68	Kyrgyzstanand Mongolia
69	Benin
70	China, São Tomé and Príncipe
71	Ivory Coast, Guinea, Marocco and Senegal
72	Burkina Faso, Haiti, Tajikistan and Uzbekistan
73	Mauritania

Place

74	Mozambique, Rwanda and Togo
75	Egypt, Gabon, Madagascar, Mali, Niger
76	Bhutan and Comoros
77	Guinea-Bissau, Cambodia, Chad, Turkmenistan and Vietnam
78	Algeria and India
79	Jordan, Laos and Liberia
80	Angola, Equatorial Guinea, Burundi, Cameroon and Central African Republic
81	Republic of the Congo
82	Nigeria
83	Djibouti
84	Democratic Republic of the Congo
85	Kosovo and Myanmar
86	Eritrea, North Korea and Palestinian Territories
87	Ethiopia, Lebanon, Sri Lanka and South Sudan
88	Bangladesh, Iran, Yemen, Libya, Nepal and Sudan
89	Somalia
90	Syria
91	Iraq
92	Pakistan
93	Afghanistan

(*quoted after: https://www.passportindex.org, June 2017)

439

© Prestel Verlag, Munich · London · New York, 2017
A member of Verlagsgruppe Random House GmbH
Neumarkter Strasse 28 · 81673 Munich

www.prestel.de

Concept: Christian Rieker
Texts: Philipp Hontschik
Translation: Rebecca van Dyck
Editor and Editorial Management: Nicola von Velsen
Research Figures: Melanie Ippach
Research and Coordination of Images: Judith Klein
Copyediting: Verlagsbüro Wais & Partner
Graphic Design: Birthe Steinbeck
Typesetting: Hilde Knauer
Production Management: Friederike Schirge
Reprographics: Reproline Mediateam
Printing and Binding: TBB a.s., Banská Bystrica
Paper: Tauro Offset
Verlagsgruppe Random House FSC® N001967

Printed in Slovakia
ISBN 978-3-7913-8373-6

In respect to links in the book, Verlagsgruppe Random
House expressly notes that no illegal content was
discernible on the linked sites at the time the links
were created. The Publisher has no influence at all
over the current and future design, content or author-
ship of the linked sites. For this reason the Publisher
expressly disassociates itself from all content on
linked sites that has been altered since the link was
created and assumes no liability for such content.

Editor's Acknowledgements
We extend our thanks to all of those individuals,
from far and near, who either themselves took
pictures of the covers of their passports for this
project—or had family members, friends, or
acquaintances do so—and sent them to us. Our
gratitude goes out to everyone who supported us
in this search and the setup of the network.

We would like to thank the Federal Foreign Office
of Germany, the Federal Police Headquarters in
Potsdam, and the European Council with its public
online register PRADO for helpful information.

Image Credits
© for all passport covers with the issuing countries
© Illustrations of passports: Abihatsira Issac/
shutterstock.com: Albania, Ethiopia, Estland,
Fidji, Latvia, Lithuania, Nigeria, Serbia, Spain,
South Africa, Togo; KUMOHD/shutterstock.com:
Malaysia; Natalya Matveeva/shutterstock.com:
Moldavia; Saman527/shutterstock.com: Sri Lanka;
Sukiyaki/shutterstock.com: Japan; Charles Taylor/
shutterstock.com: pp. 26/27, 72/73, 100/101,
202/203, 312/313, 406/407.